T0286794

Cambridge Elements ☰

Elements in Corpus Linguistics
edited by
Susan Hunston
University of Birmingham

CITATIONS IN INTERDISCIPLINARY RESEARCH ARTICLES

Natalia Muguiro
National University of La Pampa

CAMBRIDGE
UNIVERSITY PRESS

CAMBRIDGE
UNIVERSITY PRESS

University Printing House, Cambridge CB2 8BS, United Kingdom

One Liberty Plaza, 20th Floor, New York, NY 10006, USA

477 Williamstown Road, Port Melbourne, VIC 3207, Australia

314–321, 3rd Floor, Plot 3, Splendor Forum, Jasola District Centre,
New Delhi – 110025, India

79 Anson Road, #06–04/06, Singapore 079906

Cambridge University Press is part of the University of Cambridge.

It furthers the University's mission by disseminating knowledge in the pursuit of
education, learning, and research at the highest international levels of excellence.

www.cambridge.org
Information on this title: www.cambridge.org/9781108749947
DOI: 10.1017/9781108886086

First published 2020

A catalogue record for this publication is available from the British Library.

ISBN 978-1-108-74994-7 Paperback
ISSN 2632–8097 (online)
ISSN 2632–8089 (print)

Citations in Interdisciplinary Research Articles

Elements in Corpus Linguistics

DOI: 10.1017/9781108886086
First published online: November 2020

Natalia Muguiro
National University of La Pampa

Author for correspondence: nataliamuguiro@humanas.unlpam.edu.ar

Abstract: This Element explores interdisciplinarity in academic writing. It describes the ways in which disciplines interact when forming interdisciplinary fields and how language reflects (and is reflected by) these interactions. Specifically, bibliographical citations are investigated in corpora of research articles from three interdisciplines: Educational Neuroscience, Economic History, and Science and Technology Studies, as well as the single-domain disciplines from which they are derived. Comparisons are carried out between the interdisciplinary fields and between those fields and their related single-domain disciplines. The study combines analysis of quantitative data and qualitative interpretation by means of close reading. It concludes that bibliographical citations constitute a viable tool to explore interdisciplinary writing in the fields explored. The Element demonstrates that it is possible to describe epistemologically distinct types of interdisciplinarity by means of linguistic evidence.

Keywords: interdisciplinarity, academic writing, bibliographical citations, epistemological differences, linguistic variation

ISBNs: 9781108749947 (PB), 9781108886086 (OC)
ISSNs: 2632–8097 (online), 2632–8089 (print)

Contents

1 Introduction

1.1 This Element: Its Focus and Aims

At first sight, readers approaching this Element might ask themselves whether this is (yet) another corpus-based study on disciplinary variation in written academic discourse. Such a reaction might seem logical, indeed, due to the vast number of corpus-based investigations published in the last decades aimed at analyzing linguistic aspects that reflect disciplinary differences across genres, proficiency levels, or background languages and cultures. The answer, in fact, is affirmative in two ways. In the first place, this Element does report the results of a corpus-based study. In the second, this Element does refer to the analysis of written academic discourse. The third aspect of the question, however, might not have a completely affirmative answer. this Element is not entirely concerned with disciplinary variation – or, at least, not in the way such a topic has been traditionally addressed. Defined by dictionaries as "between," "among," "in the midst of," "mutually," "reciprocally," or "together," the prefix *inter-* invites reflection on how we understand academic disciplines and disciplinary knowledge. Interdisciplinarity, as defined by Graff (2015a, para. 4), focuses on "the development and application of conceptualizations, theories, sources and methods" drawn from different disciplines and aims at their integration so as to develop new approaches and solve problems in new ways.

As pointed out by Thompson and Hunston (2020), most corpus-based research on disciplinary variation has regarded disciplines as discrete, unproblematic entities. This has been so, most probably, due to the convenience of such a view for the comparative nature of those studies. This Element also takes a comparative approach; however, it rests on an understanding of academic disciplines that challenges the idea of disciplinary homogeneity and the existence of fixed disciplinary boundaries. Going back to address the initial question, this Element is focused on exploring interdisciplinarity in academic written discourse by providing readers with an understanding of the ways in which academic disciplines interact when forming interdisciplinary fields and how language reflects (and is reflected by) these interactions.

Research on the topic of interdisciplinarity is abundant. In fact, Graff (2015b) reports that between 300 and 400 articles on the subject are published each year. However, despite such efforts to understand interdisciplinarity, several conflicts and contradictions are still present. Most of them are rooted in what Graff (2015b, p. 10) has called "myths of interdisciplinarity." One of these myths is often present in studies that "reveal expectations of similarity among interdisciplines" (Graff, 2015b, p. 11). In other words, such studies are based on the myth that interdisciplines are all similar to each other. Those assumptions interfere with the need to offer comparisons of interdisciplines from diverse disciplinary clusters. Consequently, they also lead to incomplete examinations or overgeneralizations without providing sufficient evidence. Graff (2015b) further argues that more case studies and comparative studies are needed in order to demystify such assumptions. From a similar perspective, Fuchsman (2012) claims that interdisciplines are still understudied, and he also calls for more studies that serve to identify similarities and differences among interdisciplines.

In an attempt to fill this gap, the main aim of this corpus-based case study is to explore the language of research articles (RAs) from three different interdisciplinary fields: Educational Neuroscience (EN), Economic History (EH), and Science and Technology Studies (STS). These interdisciplines have originated from completely different disciplinary clusters: neuroscience and education in the first case, economics and history in the second one, and ethics, biomedicine, and computer engineering in the third one. A second, related aim is to compare interdisciplinary with monodisciplinary writing in an attempt to find out if typical language features of interdisciplinary writing can be identified as well as to study the degree of influence from one or the other single-domain fields over each interdiscipline. In order to reach this second aim, the monodisciplines that interact in each case will be analyzed in comparison with each corresponding interdiscipline. The work reported in this Element is focused on the use of bibliographical citations. The reasons for this choice, as well as other theoretical and methodological aspects, will be discussed in the sections that follow so as to provide the general background for this study.

1.2 Why Interdisciplinarity?

Interdisciplinarity is a ubiquitous term in current academic and educational settings, and it is rapidly becoming a dominant form of scholarly work (Graff, 2015b; Barry and Born, 2013). This scenario, however, has generated a heated debate about what is meant by interdisciplinarity. In order to shed some light, I will start by clarifying the understanding of interdisciplinarity in this Element.

According to Graff (2015b, p. 5), interdisciplinarity "is part of the historical making and ongoing reshaping of modern disciplines." Interdisciplinarity is inseparable from disciplinarity but not oppositional to it. In other words, disciplinary and interdisciplinary work are inextricably linked and mutually dependent (Graff, 2015a). As stated before, interdisciplinarity is defined and constructed by several problems and questions as well as by the means to answer those questions in different and also in new ways. This emphasis on solving problems is often linked to the contemporary pressures and threats encountered in the real world. (Graff, 2015b).

Another important point of agreement among theoreticians is the fact that there is "no single path to interdisciplinarity, no single model, no single standard for successful development" (Graff, 2015b, p. 5). In these terms, interdisciplinarity must be understood "less as a unity and more as a field of differences," as argued by Barry and Born (2013, p. 15). A final consideration is that interdisciplinarity not only consists of the integration of various kinds of disciplinary knowledge but also comprises "the challenges surrounding effective communication to different audiences" (Frodeman et al., 2017, p. 38). In sum, this work is underpinned by an idea of interdisciplinarity as a historical construct aimed at addressing questions and problems that have consequences in the real world. In addition, the idea of *difference* is a central one: there are different types of interdisciplinarity and different types of audiences.

1.2.1 Understanding Disciplinarity in the Context of Interdisciplinarity

To grasp the true essence of interdisciplinarity, a definition of *academic discipline* that is suitable for such understanding should be proposed. This conception of discipline, as stated before, needs to challenge the idea of disciplinary homogeneity. On top of that, it also needs to challenge the existence of fixed disciplinary boundaries as a rigid notion and to leave some room for their crossing. The definition provided by Trowler et al. (2012), which is built on a social practice perspective, might constitute an adequate starting point. According to the authors, disciplines are:

> Reservoirs of knowledge resources shaping regularized behavioral practices, sets of discourses, ways of thinking, procedures, emotional responses and motivations. These provide structured dispositions for disciplinary practitioners who reshape them in different practice clusters into localized repertoires. While alternative recurrent practices may be in competition within a single discipline, there is common background knowledge about key figures, conflicts and achievements. Disciplines take organizational form, have internal hierarchies and bestow power differentially, conferring advantage and disadvantage. (Trowler et al., 2012, p. 9)

The most noticeable merit of this definition is that, as acknowledged by its authors, it "allows for the division and conflict we see within most disciplines, but also recognizes that there is a degree of commonality" (Trowler et al., 2012, p. 9). Moreover, the fact that disciplines might vary according to context is also pointed out. This definition, however, needs to be complemented by the understanding that no clear lines or boundaries between disciplines can be drawn, as argued by Weingart and Sterhr (2000, p. xi): "The organizational matrix of disciplines is beginning to dissolve [...]. Disciplinary interests, boundaries, and constraints are dissolving and disciplines are merging in areas where their overlap forms a new field."

This image of more blurred disciplinary boundaries is rooted in a series of spatial metaphors that have historically been applied to describe academic disciplines. In their well-known work, which has been highly influential and widely used in discourse studies of disciplinary variation, Becher and Trowler (2001), based on Biglan (1973), describe disciplines as *academic tribes* that occupy different *disciplinary territories*. The ways in which "academics engage with their subject matter" (the tribal part) are "important structural factors in the formulation of disciplinary cultures" (the territorial part) (Becher and Trowler, 2001, p. 23). The authors add the area of application to their model, and, accordingly, they propose a system of four knowledge domains: "hard-pure" (physics, chemistry, etc.), "soft-pure" (history, anthropology, etc.), "hard-applied" (medicine, engineering, etc.), and "soft-applied" (education, law, etc.) (Becher and Trowler, 2001, p. 35).

Although this *tribes-and-territories* metaphor has been extensively used, it has also been an object of sound criticism. Trowler (2012) himself argued, a decade later, that "more fluid metaphors" are required, as drawing clear lines between disciplines and using images of "fields," "boundaries," "territories," "tribes," and so on is unhelpful (Trowler, 2012, p. 11). According to his even more recent criticism towards these essentialist views of disciplines, Trowler (2013) points out that each individual discipline has no essential "core characteristics" in the sense of being "all present and identifiable at all times" (Trowler, 2013, p. 4); this is consistent with the definition of *academic discipline* provided at the beginning of this section.

Along the same lines, Manathunga and Brew (2012, p. 65) propose leaving aside "land-based" metaphors such as *territories* so as to explore disciplinarity in terms of *oceans* and to see knowledge domains in terms of *fluidity*. Similarly, Martin (2011) talks of embarking through interdisciplinary *troubled waters*. Furthermore, Manathunga and Brew (2012, p. 67) point out that although Becher and Trowler's (2001) description of academic communities as *tribes* still persists, references to *academic cultures* are becoming more common instead. This is the term Kagan (2009) uses when he skillfully describes the three cultures: the culture of the natural sciences, the culture of the social sciences, and the culture of the humanities.

As a conclusion, and leaving the controversies around essentialist taxonomies aside, the necessity of acknowledging disciplinary differences cannot be ignored. Disciplines are inherently different in terms of their subject matter, how they conceptualize knowledge, the methods they use, and the types of results they obtain. However, because disciplines are better conceptualized as fluid entities that do not have fixed boundaries, they have more in common with oceans than with territories. This view is thus in agreement with the idea of interdisciplinarity underlying this work.

1.2.2 Forms of Interdisciplinarity

The common approach in most previous research on disciplinary variation in academic discourse has been to analyze certain language features in a selection of disciplines to be compared (Hyland, 2000; Biber et al., 2002; Charles, 2003; Silver, 2003; Groom, 2005; Harwood, 2005; Peacock, 2014; among many others). Results are then interpreted in terms of the categorization of such disciplines within available taxonomies. The rationale underlying these studies is that each domain reflects a discipline-specific academic culture based on "shared codes of conduct, sets of values and distinctive intellectual tasks" (Becher, 1981, p. 109) in line with what has been traditionally understood as *disciplinary discourse* (Becher, 1987). When linguistic features are studied in interdisciplinary fields, however, this rationale cannot be applied any longer. In this different scenario, while it is important to consider what is already known about disciplinary differences, it is even more important to understand how disciplines interact when forming heterogeneous interdisciplinary fields; that is, when new interdisciplinary fields are created and become disciplines themselves. In other words, new theoretical frameworks need to be developed based on interdisciplinary epistemological values so as to describe linguistic aspects that reflect disciplinary **interaction** rather than solely disciplinary **variation**.

Interdisciplinarity is commonly understood as a response to disciplinary structures of knowledge. This response, Welch (2011) claims, necessarily involves epistemology, since disciplines not only organize knowledge but also establish norms of validation and the languages through which disciplinary investigation is conducted. In fact, one of the most noticeable contrasts between disciplinarity and interdisciplinarity is that they adopt completely different approaches regarding epistemology (Repko and Szostak, 2017). As each disciplinary perspective involves a set of epistemological attitudes towards knowing and describing reality (by answering questions such as "what can we know?" and "how can we know it?"), interdisciplinarity must necessarily respect these various epistemologies. As a result, interdisciplinarity is distinguished by its "epistemological pluralism" (Repko and Szostak, 2017, p. 21). Epistemological pluralism rejects notions of absolute truth and advocates for the ambiguity produced by conflict and difference. In this way, knowledge emerges from the interaction of different epistemological perspectives (Repko and Szostak, 2017). Framed by its epistemological pluralism, interdisciplinarity has been described as adopting particular forms that are influenced by a number of factors, such as the nature of the disciplines involved, the extent to which they are integrated, and the relationship between them. As a result, several taxonomies have been proposed that frame different analytical models (see Klein, 2017 for a complete description).

For the purposes of this Element, a framework has been developed that focuses on the description of *contrasting types* (Klein, 2017) and distinct *modes* (Barry and Born, 2013) of interdisciplinarity. Contrasting typologies (Klein, 2017) are useful in exploring the nature of the disciplines involved and their degrees of integration when forming interdisciplines. Three contrasting pairs – that is, *bridge-building vs. restructuring, hybridization vs. borrowing,* and *critical vs. instrumental* – will be considered in Section 3 to compare monodisciplinary with interdisciplinary writing. As for the relationship between the disciplines involved, three modes of interdisciplinarity, defined as "ideal-typical arrangements of the interrelations between disciplines," will be explored: the *subordination-service*, the "integrative synthesis," and the *agonistic-antagonistic* modes (Barry and Born, 2013). These will constitute the framework for the comparison between interdisciplines in Section 4.

Finally, it is of paramount importance to point out that the interdisciplinary fields that make up the corpus of this work were chosen *a priori* because they are very different from an **epistemological** point of view, and so might be expected to represent different types and distinct modes of interdisciplinarity. However, the focus of this research is placed on demonstrating whether these fields are also different *a posteriori*, from a **linguistic** point of view.

1.2.3 Disciplines and Interdisciplinary Mixtures

As one of the main aims of this study is to compare interdisciplines, the focus is placed on exploring those in which the disciplines involved are different in nature from each other. On top of that, the three interdisciplines need to be different as regards the kind of disciplinary mixture involved.

As already stated, Educational Neuroscience (EN), Economic History (EH), and Science and Technology Studies (STS) are the three interdisciplinary fields chosen to study in this work. In the case of Educational Neuroscience, the two disciplines that make up the mixture are education (EDU) and neuroscience (NEU) (a branch of biology also called neurobiology). Education shares the culture of the *social sciences*, while neuroscience is a *natural science* (Kagan, 2009). For ease of reference, Educational Neuroscience and its two related disciplines form Set 1. As regards Economic History, the mixture is between another *social science*, economics (ECO) in this case, and history (HIS), which is a *humanity* (Kagan, 2009). Economic History and its two related disciplines form Set 2. In the case of Science and Technology Studies, as this is an interdisciplinary field that covers a wide variety of topical subfields (Jasanoff, 2017), two different, although related, disciplines have been selected. More specifically, when biomedicine (BIO), which is defined as the branch of medical sciences that applies biological and physiological principles to clinical practice, is in contact with ethics (ETH) (a branch of philosophy), issues within the area of bioethics arise. In the same fashion, when computer engineering (ENG), defined as the branch of engineering that integrates several fields of computer science and electronics engineering, also interacts with ethics (ETH), engineering ethics topics arise. Bioethical and engineering ethics issues are only two of the several topical subfields that Science and Technology Studies encompasses. In other words, biomedicine and computer engineering, which are *technologies* or *applied sciences* (Gardner, 1995), in combination with ethics, which is another *humanity* (Kagan, 2009), merge to form two topical areas from the broader interdisciplinary field of Science and Technology Studies. This field and its three related disciplines form Set 3.

1.2.4 Interdisciplines and Their Journals

The three interdisciplines under analysis are defined in the paragraphs that follow according to descriptions provided in their journals. It is important to make it clear that a journal may be defined as *interdisciplinary* in a general sense, that is, like journals that "publish articles from across multiple disciplines," which "are often outside of one's own discipline" or which may or may not be "located within one discipline but cater to a wide array of disciplines or fields" (Afifi, 2017, p. 758). The interdisciplinary journals selected for this study, however, fit a more specific description: they are interdisciplinary in the sense that the interdisciplines they represent explicitly combine two disciplines. In other words, the existence of such journals reifies the interdisciplines as such, gives them identity, and legitimizes their knowledge as interdisciplinary autonomous fields. Once each journal has been presented, each interdiscipline is analyzed from the perspective of the modes of interdisciplinarity proposed by Barry and Born (2013) and according to the contrasting types of interdisciplinarity illustrated by Klein (2017).

Educational Neuroscience

Educational Neuroscience, as defined by Patten and Campbell (2011, p. 1), involves "syntheses of theories, methods, and techniques of the neurosciences, as applied to and informed by educational research and practice." *Mind, Brain, & Education* and *Trends in Neuroscience and Education* are the journals selected for analysis. The journal *Mind, Brain, & Education*[1] aims at "supporting the development of a framework for new ideas to advance research efforts at the intersection of biology, brain, cognition, and education, and the practical innovations these research efforts inform." *Trends in Neuroscience and Education*[2], the other journal, proposes "to bridge the gap between the increasing basic cognitive and neuroscience understanding of learning and the application of this knowledge in educational settings."

This bridging-the-gap metaphor is inherent to the field, whose ultimate goal is to bridge education and neuroscience (Campbell, 2011). Thus, from the typologies illustrated by Klein (2017), the contrast between the *bridge-building* and the *restructuring* types is useful. Bridge-building occurs between complete and firm disciplines, while restructuring detaches parts of several disciplines to form a new coherent whole. In restructuring processes, traditional disciplinary categories are questioned and their boundaries are blurred. In bridge-building typologies, however, traditional categories of knowledge remain intact.

Educational Neuroscience can be described as sharing more aspects of the bridge-building typology than of the restructuring one, despite the continuous effort made by education and neuroscience researchers and practitioners to fill the gap between one and the other sides of the bridge. Edelenbosch et al. (2015, p. 48) interviewed neuroscientists and education professionals about their perceptions as regards this gap. They concluded that if neuroscience is to contribute to the complex and value-laden practice of education, it is time to find the "middle road between scientific rigor and the more pragmatic approach of the field of education," although they acknowledge this as a difficult process, since it cannot be expected that scientists and educators will make this radical shift overnight.

In addition, as pointed out in the *Trends in Neuroscience and Education* journal, "neuroscience is to education what biology is to medicine and physics is to architecture." This appreciation has to do more with the hierarchical division of labor that characterizes many forms of interdisciplinarity. In fact, it serves to characterize Educational Neuroscience as fitting one of the interdisciplinary modes proposed by Barry and Born (2013, p. 25): the *subordination-service* mode. According to this, one or more disciplines occupies a subordinate or service role in relation to the other disciplines involved, and "the service

---

[1] https://onlinelibrary.wiley.com/journal/1751228x

[2] www.journals.elsevier.com/trends-in-neuroscience-and-education

discipline(s) are typically conceived as making up for, or filling in for, an absence or lack in the other, (master) discipline(s)." In this case, education lacks the knowledge provided by neuroscience (master discipline), but neuroscience needs to be informed by education (service discipline) in order to fulfil the aims of the interdisciplinary activity.

Economic History

As stated by Shanahan (2015), it is not simple to define the boundaries of Economic History. There are multiple intersections and overlaps with other fields. For this study, the *Journal of Economic History* and the *Economic History Review* are the journals selected for analysis. In the *Journal of Economic History*[3], it is noted that Economic History "is devoted to the multidisciplinary study of history and economics, and is of interest not only to economic historians but to social and demographic historians, as well as economists in general." The second journal, the *Economic History Review*[4], aims to "keep anyone interested in economic and social history abreast of current developments in the subject." While Economic History draws extensively on its close relationships with the disciplines of economics and history, its ultimate strength lies in its broad interdisciplinary connections across a wide range of social science and business subjects. Furthermore, it encourages diverse but rigorous approaches to understand our economic past. In most cases, there is a productive "cross-fertilization" process between history and economics (Ritter and Horn, 1986, p. 439).

This cross-fertilization process helps to characterize Economic History within the contrasting types of *borrowing* vs. *hybridization* illustrated by Klein (2017). Borrowing is more typical of methodological interdisciplinarities; that is, borrowing a method or concept from another discipline to test a hypothesis, to answer a research question, or to help develop a theory (Bruun et al., 2005, p. 84). Hybridization, however, encompasses a general process of development with two stages: the first is specialization and the second is the continuous reintegration of fragments and specialties. It is clear that Economic History goes beyond the borrowing of methods and concepts from one discipline or the other. In fact, it has been described as a hybrid or "interstitial cross-discipline" (Klein, 2017, p. 27). Klein (1996, p. 192) understands interdisciplines like Economic History as "institutionalized hybrid fields" and distinguishes them from mere disciplinary exchanges that

---

[3] www.cambridge.org/core/journals/journal-of-economic-history
[4] https://onlinelibrary.wiley.com/journal/14680289

remain at the level of cross-disciplinary contacts and borrowing of methods and concepts.

Finally, a suitable way to understand the relationship between the disciplinary forms of knowledge that interact in Economic History is to think of them as part of a synthesis through a process of integration or negotiation, typical of an *integrative-synthesis* (Barry and Born, 2013) mode of interdisciplinarity. According to this mode, a given interdisciplinary practice "proceeds through the integration of two or more disciplines in relatively symmetrical form" (Barry and Born, 2013, p. 25): mainly economics and history in this case. In other words, interdisciplinarity is understood additively as the sum of two or more disciplinary components or as achieved through a synthesis of different disciplinary approaches, as suggested by Petts et al. (2008).

Science and Technology Studies

Science and Technology Studies is "an interdisciplinary field that investigates the institutions, practices, meanings, and outcomes of science and technology and their multiple entanglements with the world's people inhabit, their lives, and their values" (Felt et al., 2017, p. 1). More specifically, Science and Technology Studies involves two broad streams of scholarship: a focus on the nature and practices of science and technology and an emphasis on the impact, control, and risks that science and technology pose to human values (Jasanoff, 2017). This latter stream frames the scope of the selected journals: *Science, Technology, & Human Values* and *Science and Engineering Ethics*. Both publish articles about bioethical issues and the ethical dimension of engineering. As the editors of *Science, Technology, & Human Values*[5] point out, scientific advances improve our lives, but they also complicate how we live and react to the new technologies. As a result, human values come into conflict with scientific advancement. Furthermore, research that examines ethical issues that arise from the practice of science and engineering is needed in order to cope with instances of misconduct in science, as stated by the editors of the *Science and Engineering Ethics*[6] journal.

In short, Science and Technology Studies research "seeks to open up science, technology, and society to critical assessment and interrogation" (Felt et al., 2017, p. 1). For Jasanoff (2017, p. 192), this field "problematizes the notion of discipline and stresses the idea of challenging disciplinary configurations." Such a description helps to characterize this interdiscipline as a *critical* type, which contrasts with the *instrumental* type (Klein, 2017). According to Repko and Szostak (2017), instrumental interdisciplinarity is problem-driven. It is

---

[5] https://journals.sagepub.com/home/sth [6] https://www.springer.com/journal/11948

a pragmatic approach that focuses on research, borrowing, and practical problem-solving in response to the external demands of society. Critical interdisciplinarity, on the contrary, is society driven. It "interrogates the dominant structure of knowledge with the aim of transforming it, while raising epistemological and political questions of value and purpose" (Klein, 2010, p. 30). Critical interdisciplinarians fault the instrumentalists for "merely combining existing disciplinary approaches without advocating their transformation" (Klein, 2005, pp. 57–8).

As regards the modes of interdisciplinarity proposed by Barry and Born (2013), Science and Technology Studies might position itself in an *agonistic-antagonistic* fashion, as suggested by Jasanoff (2013, p. 100), both "within its own emerging boundaries and in relation to the intellectual territories occupied by other disciplines." In this case, these include the sciences and technologies, which constitute the particular topics of study, and the social sciences and humanities, which are used to represent the social realities studied (Jasanoff, 2013). Interdisciplinarity, then, is driven by an agonistic or antagonistic relation to existing forms of disciplinary knowledge.

As explained before, the disciplines that interact in the three interdisciplines are different in nature, but also the kind of interaction between them is different. These features have been illustrated in the following diagram (Figure 1.1), where disciplines of the same nature share the same color and

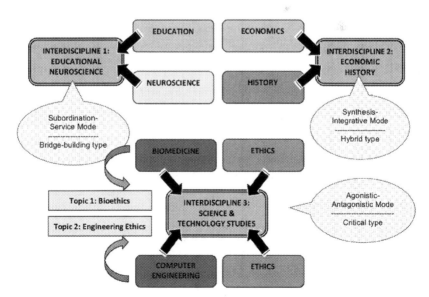

Figure 1.1 Description of the disciplines and interdisciplines and their relationships in the corpus

arrows indicate the resulting interdiscipline for each set. Furthermore, as has just been described, each interdiscipline might represent a different mode of interdisciplinarity as well as show elements that permit us to characterize them according to different types. Both modes and types have been included in the diagram by means of speech bubbles.

1.2.5 Previous Corpus-Based Research on Interdisciplinarity in Academic Discourse

Hood (2011) argues that by understanding the ways in which disciplines use language differently, we can provide meaningful support for research across disciplinary boundaries, as is the aim of this study. As stated before, previous corpus-based research on academic discourse and disciplinary variation mostly focuses on the description of linguistic features across different disciplines, as reviewed by Hyland and Bondi (2006), among others. In comparison, relatively little research has been published to date on the study of interdisciplinary discourse, and corpus-based studies in particular are similarly scarce.

Exceptions to this are Thompson and Hunston's (2020) book on interdisciplinary research discourse and Choi and Richards' (2017) volume on spoken communication in interdisciplinary research contexts; these indicate that the topic carries an enormous potential for future research. Thompson and Hunston (2020) apply a variety of text-based and corpus-based methods to investigate the language of research articles in interdisciplinary journals. They aim to show that what is known about interdisciplinary epistemology can be reflected in the language of such journals (also see Murakami et al., 2017; Thompson et al., 2017). As for the study of spoken interdisciplinary discourse, Choi and Richards (2017) analyze recorded interactions between researchers from different disciplines and identify opportunities and difficulties involved in interdisciplinary engagement. They discuss the results in the light of their usefulness in informing interdisciplinary practice.

An earlier corpus-based study looking into the topic of interdisciplinarity in academic discourse was conducted by Oakey et al. (2011), who compared the interdisciplinary field of health and social care and its contributory disciplines, medicine and social work, by looking at collocations with prepositions. They argued that the words occurring near prepositions can reveal methodological and epistemological aspects of the fields. Similarly, Teich and Holtz (2009) studied the lexico-grammatical contexts of selected nouns in two disciplines, linguistics and computer sciences, in comparison with the interdisciplinary field of computational linguistics, to assess their contribution to register formation. This Element is similar to the studies by Teich and Holtz (2009) and Oakey et al.

(2011) in the sense that it also compares single-domain disciplines with the resulting interdisciplines. It is different, however, in the sense that it additionally offers comparisons between interdisciplines. Furthermore, there is an explicit intention here to contextualize and interpret the results obtained in the light of the values of epistemological pluralism and interdisciplinary complexity.

1.3 Why Bibliographical Citations?

As simply put by Charles (2006, p. 311), citation plays a key role in academic writing because "it shows how a new piece of research arises out of and is grounded in the current state of disciplinary knowledge." Furthermore, bibliographical citations are also central because they help to provide justification and evidence for arguments and claims to demonstrate familiarity with the literature (Hyland, 2000). As citations carry rhetorical and social meanings that are represented by the choices writers make, they help writers to establish a persuasive stance, since "new work has to be embedded in a community-generated literature to demonstrate its relevance and importance" (Hyland, 2000, p. 22). In short, writers introduce and discuss the contributions of other researchers and scholars, and by showing knowledge displays of previous research they "establish membership in the relevant disciplinary community" (Swales, 2014, p. 119).

Abundant work has been carried out on the examination of citation practices in academic writing. Since the 1980s, many scholars have viewed citations as useful resources for rhetorical purposes (Swales, 1986; 1990; Dudley-Evans, 1986; Hopkins and Dudley-Evans, 1988; Berkenkotter and Huckin, 1995; Myers, 1990). In addition, cross-disciplinary variation has been widely studied (Hyland, 1999; 2000; Thompson, 2005; Charles, 2006), as well as variation according to genre (Thompson and Tribble, 2001), language and culture (Atkinson, 2004; Fløttum et al., 2006; Hu and Wang, 2014), and the language proficiency level of the writers (Petrić, 2012; Lee et al., 2018). Furthermore, several aspects like citation density (Hyland, 1999; 2000; Thompson and Tribble, 2001; Thompson, 2005; Fløttum et al., 2006; Coffin, 2009), rhetorical functions (Harwood, 2009; Harwood and Petrić, 2012; 2013), writer stance (Coffin, 2009), or reporting verbs (Thompson and Ye, 1991; Hunston, 1993; Thomas and Hawes, 1994; Hyland, 2000; Bloch, 2010) have been specifically explored. In this Element, most of these and other previous studies have been taken into account to interpret the results obtained and to build the analytical framework adopted.

1.4 Hypotheses and Research Questions

In interdisciplinary academic writing, citations play the same central role described above, with the additional need to support the purpose of interdisciplinary journals and articles. Thompson (2015) defines an interdisciplinary research journal from the perspective of the intended readership. He states that "it is a journal in which researchers from a range of disciplines write papers for an audience that is similarly composed of researchers from a broad range of disciplines." In comparison with articles from disciplinary journals, in articles published in interdisciplinary journals writers "draw on a broader range of literature" to situate the research and to demonstrate its applicability beyond their own discipline (Centre for Corpus Research, 2017, p. 7).

In this Element, it is hypothesized that if citations are more varied in interdisciplinary writing, it is likely that they also need to be similarly or even more frequent than in monodisciplinary writing. Moreover, it is expected that interdisciplinary journals will show citation practices that are typical of their constituent disciplines.

Based on these hypotheses as well as on the theoretical considerations presented in this introductory section, the following research questions have been proposed:

RQ 1 What evidence is there that citation practices in the interdisciplines are drawn from those in the single-domain disciplines?

RQ 2 How does the use of bibliographical citations differ across the three interdisciplines?

1.5 Outline of This Element

This Element is organized as follows. Section 2 deals with the description of the corpus and the methodology. After that, Section 3 focuses on comparing the single-domain disciplines with the interdisciplines formed. For that, the issue of citation density is considered first. Then, the focus is placed on the distinction between integral and nonintegral citations as well as the difference between attributed and averred sources. Section 4 is aimed at comparing the three interdisciplines, and the scope is reduced to the analysis of the cases in which citations convey attribution only. For that, the grammatical structures used, the processes of textual integration applied, and the reporting verbs employed are studied. Finally, in Section 5, some general conclusions are presented.

2 Corpus and Methodology

2.1 Description of the Corpus

The corpus in this study is divided into ten sub-corpora of research articles (RAs) published in different monodisciplinary and interdisciplinary scientific journals. Considerations about the choice of genre, the selection of journals, and the sampling of texts, as well as corpus design issues, are presented in the following sections.

2.1.1 Genre

The decision to study RAs is grounded in the fact that, as Canagarajah (2002, pp. 32–3) affirms, there is consensus among recognized scholars that "the journal article is the primary mode of validating their research findings." Such is the status of RAs that academic communities depend on them to legitimate new knowledge across fields (Canagarajah, 2002). Along the same lines, Charles and Pecorari (2016, p. 176) point out that RAs occupy a special status in the English for Academic Purposes (EAP) area, since they represent "the most thoroughly researched expert genre" and constitute an "extremely prestigious form of publication across the university." As the main aim of this work is to study interdisciplinarity in academic writing, to study RAs means to study the type of text that is most significantly valued by academic writers and their research communities. As pointed out by Thompson and Hunston (2020), research from the 1990s has made clear that disciplinary communities and individual identities are construed according to how research is reported by means of academic writing (Halliday and Martin, 1993; Hunston, 1994; Swales, 1990; 2004; Hyland, 2012).

2.1.2 Selection of Journals and Sampling of Texts

The main criterion for journal selection was to choose the most influential or prestigious journals across the range of disciplines. Eleven of the thirteen journals are registered in the Journal Citation Reports (JCR), which is one the most authoritative tools used by the academic community to identify the most important journals based on their impact factor (IF). Furthermore, searches were made through the Scimago Journal Rank system (based on information from Scopus) so as to make sure that the journals chosen were ranked between the first and the twenty-fifth positions in each field. However, an additional criterion for the selection of the topical monodisciplinary journals from Set 3 (Science and Technology Studies and their related disciplines) was considered. As the two selected journals from Science and Technology Studies deal with only two specific topics or areas (bioethics and engineering ethics) within the broad spectrum that this particular interdisciplinary field offers, the selection of the journals that represent the single-domain disciplines (biomedicine and computer engineering) was based more on the representativeness of the topics covered than on the prestige of the journals selected. For this reason, these are the only two journals that are not registered in the JCR index. However, both journals report high-impact values based on other metrics, such as the Scientific Journal Impact Factor (SJIF) or the Source Normalized Impact per Paper (SNIP).

As regards the sampling of the texts, the aim was to include the most recent RAs published in each selected journal. In order to do so, the search was started from the most recent journal issues available, whose tables of contents were examined. Texts such as editorials, book reviews, letters, etc. were excluded and only the RAs were collected. In some journals, labels other than Research Article were used, such as Original Articles or just Articles. In such cases, the texts were skimmed to check that they had the structure of RAs and reported new knowledge claims or brought contributions to the field. As regards year of publication, all the sampled articles were published between 2007 and 2017. It should be noted, however, that because the journals were not alike in the number of RAs published each year, the number of texts from the same year also differs. Examples of citations taken from the RAs in the corpus have been included in every section of this Element to illustrate different linguistic aspects, and their corresponding bibliographical references have been provided in Appendix 1.

Finally, when articles were stored and prepared for corpus-based analysis, they were first retrieved in their electronic versions as PDF or HTML files, and they were then converted into plain text files (Unicode format) by using the AntFileConverter (Anthony, 2017) software tools. Then the abstracts, acknowledgments, explanatory footnotes or endnotes, appendices, and lists of references were removed from the texts. As for the computer-based identification and retrieval of citations processes, which are described in detail in Section 2.2.3, the AntCont (Anthony, 2018) software was used, a freeware toolkit for concordancing and corpus analysis of written texts.

2.1.3 Corpus Design

Four hundred and fifty (450) complete RAs were collected to build the corpus, which comprises a total of 3,309,307 running words. Every sub-corpus for the interdisciplinary fields is made up of fifty articles from two different journals (twenty-five from each journal), and every sub-corpus for the single-domain disciplines is made of fifty articles too. Thus collecting the same number of texts in each sub-corpus, rather than reaching the same number of words, was the adopted criterion to create comparable sub-corpora. This was based on similar decisions from authoritative previous research on citations in academic writing (Hyland, 1999; 2000; Thompson, 2001; Thompson and Tribble, 2001; Charles, 2006; Fløttum et al., 2006; Hu and Wang, 2014; among others). In the cases of five of the single-domain disciplines (education, neuroscience, economics, history, and ethics), the fifty RAs are all from the same journal in each field. In the case of the other two (biomedicine and computer engineering), twenty-five articles from each discipline have been collected to make the two topical sub-corpora. However, depending on the purpose of the analysis, the fifty articles have sometimes been blended together as representative of the same sub-corpus. The number of word tokens for each sub-corpus in each set is detailed in Table 2.1.

Table 2.1 Description of the corpus according to journal name, number of texts, and number of words

Discipline	Journal name	Texts	Words
Neuroscience	*Neuroscience*	50	232,092
Education	*International Journal of Educational Research*	50	318,513
Educational Neuroscience	*Trends in Neuroscience and Education* *Mind, Brain, & Education*	25 25	143,995 131,471
Total Set 1		150	826,071
Economics	*Quarterly Journal of Economics*	50	607,852
History	*Journal of Contemporary History*	50	462,631
Economic History	*Journal of Economic History* *Economic History Review*	25 25	208,415 207,647
Total Set 2		150	1,486,545
Ethics	*Ethics*	50	549,235
Biomedicine	*Biology and Medicine*	25	48,336
Computer engineering	*International Journal of Advanced Research in Computer Engineering & Technology*	25	59,017
Science and Technology Studies	*Science and Engineering Ethics* *Science, Technology, & Human Values*	25 25	171,688 168,315
Total Set 3		150	996,591
Total corpus		450	3,309,207

The corpus of this study can be defined as a *specialized small* corpus (Koester, 2010). It is specialized because it is a corpus of texts of a particular type, the RA in this case, and it is used "to investigate a particular type of language," which is academic writing in this case (Hunston, 2002, p. 14). Specialized corpora are usually smaller in scale than general language corpora due to the precision of their narrower focus precisely. However, this is not seen as a problem because the greater homogeneity of the texts in the specialized area "confers the advantage of fewer texts being required for the corpus to be representative of that language variety" (Lee, 2010, p. 114). As Koester (2010, p. 67) points out, the advantage of small specialized corpora is that they allow "a much closer link between the corpus and the contexts in which the texts in the corpus were produced." While very large corpora allow for insights into the linguistic features of language as a whole, smaller specialized corpora allow for insights into features of language use in particular settings. Furthermore, the quantitative data obtained from corpus analysis can be more easily complemented with qualitative interpretation, as shown in this study.

As a matter of size, according to Flowerdew (2004), any written corpus under five million words is considered small. However, many small corpora are a great deal smaller than that (Koester, 2010), and there is a general agreement that small corpora have up to 250,000 words (Flowerdew, 2004), which is the case for most of the sub-corpora in this study. Furthermore, the size of the corpus also depends on representativeness issues. In this regard, both situational and linguistic variability (Biber, 1993) need to be considered. Biber (1990) states that linguistic representativeness (the range of linguistic distributions) depends first of all on situational representativeness (which is quite straightforward in this study, since all samples belong to the same text type, i.e. they are all RAs) but also "on the number of words per text sample, and number of samples per register or genre included in the corpus," as Koester summarizes (2010, p. 70). By running a number of statistical tests, Biber (1990) discovered that the most common linguistic features are relatively stable in their occurrence across 1,000-word samples, and he found out that the linguistic tendencies are quite stable with ten text samples per genre or register, as also summarized by Koester (2010). However, and based on previous findings from corpus-based research on the topic, as bibliographical citations are not as frequent as the most common linguistic features (e.g. personal pronouns, contractions, past and present tense, and prepositions [Biber, 1993]), the corpus collected is bigger as regards both number of words and number of texts so as to be more representative of the linguistic aspects studied.

Finally, it is important to highlight the fact that, when designing a small specialized corpus, it is not possible "to evaluate representativeness entirely objectively" (Tognini-Bonelli, 2001, p. 57). In this particular case, the degree of linguistic variability within each discipline is not known, and neither is the extent to which each discipline is representative of its type. Furthermore, this corpus is not intended to be representative of interdisciplinary research articles as a whole. Rather, it is intended to provide data for a case study (see Section 2.2), and as such, the corpus can be considered adequate for its purpose.

2.2 Description of the Methodology

According to Hunston (2002, p. 2), the word *corpus* is used to describe "a collection of naturally occurring examples of language" consisting of collections of texts or parts of texts that are stored electronically, which have been collected for linguistic study. A corpus is defined in terms of both its form and its purpose, and, although it provides information, it cannot give interpretation. In other words, the corpus offers the researcher countless examples, but it is the researcher who has to interpret them (Hunston, 2002). Following these lines, this work has been carried out through the combination of quantitative and qualitative corpus-based methods. In essence, this combination refers to the movement backwards and forwards between the analysis of quantitative data and their qualitative interpretation by means of close reading. As pointed out by several researchers (Carter, 2004; O'Keeffe, 2006; O'Keeffe et al., 2007), combining automatic corpus analytic techniques with more fine-grained qualitative investigation constitutes a reliable methodology for dealing with the complexity of language. In sum, this means that the quantitative findings revealed by corpus analysis always need to be complemented with qualitative interpretations (Flowerdew, 2004). Moving more specifically into the techniques, very traditional corpus investigation tools have been used, namely exploring concordance lines and calculating frequencies. Concerning the approach adopted, this research follows a top-down one, since corpus searches were restricted to bibliographical citations only.

As regards its scope, this work can be defined as a *case study*, understood as "an in-depth study of one or more cases" (Duff, 2018, p. 307). By choosing just one or a small number of cases of a phenomenon, the researcher is able "to explore the phenomenon holistically and in context and can examine the complex constellation of factors involved" (Duff, 2018, p. 305). Case study research carries a prominent status and has an important role in many disciplines, including applied linguistics, where it is increasingly used in qualitative or in mixed method (qualitative/quantitative) studies (Duff, 2018).

Several possible designs for case studies and types of cases are available. Thus it is very important to define what the case is. According to Stake (1995), the case normally has "intrinsic value as an interesting exemplar of the category from which it is drawn," as well as "instrumental value in helping us understand broader issues and experiences" (Duff, 2018, p. 308). For the context of this work, each of the three interdisciplines with its respective journals only represents a case within the broader area of interdisciplinarity and interdisciplinary writing. This basically means that only three cases from all the existing interdisciplinary fields have been studied. Therefore, the findings from these cases cannot count as valid for the representation of all other interdisciplines or for interdisciplinary academic writing in general. In other words, as highlighted by Merriam (2009), a case refers to "a single bounded unit, entity or system that is the focus of inquiry within its wider frame of reference" (Duff, 2018, p. 309). Going back to the issue of representativeness, while it might be expected that the corpus is somehow representative of the selected journals, no conclusions can be drawn on what other interdisciplines show in terms of citations. As Duff (2018) concludes, case studies in applied linguistics and language education tend to seek a deeper understanding of phenomena based on data rather than to generate universal truths.

2.2.1 Variation across Journals from the Same Interdiscipline

As abundant previous research exists on the study of citations across single-domain disciplines, the RAs from the monodisciplinary sub-corpora all come from the same journal, since variation issues have been already considered in previous works. As explained in Section 2.1.3, however, the RAs from each interdisciplinary field were taken from two different journals. This has been done for two reasons. On the one hand, as there are no previous studies on citation practices in interdisciplinary fields, it was thought important to select articles from more than one journal in order to make the sample somewhat broader in scope, since no comparisons could be made with similar corpora from previous studies. On the other hand, comparing two journals from the same interdisciplinary field is useful for exploring the degree of internal journal homogeneity or heterogeneity as regards the occurrence of the linguistic features studied. Following these considerations, when citation density rates were calculated, findings from the interdisciplinary journals were reported first as wholes but also separately according to the journal. As a result, the problem of possible *local densities* (Moon, 1998) was taken into account. In the context of this work, this phenomenon is concerned with the possibility that citations would be more or less frequent in the interdisciplinary fields simply because they occur more or less frequently in only one of the journals.

2.2.2 Variation across Texts in Interdisciplinary Journals

Another important aspect taken into consideration was the range and dispersion of the citations across every individual text from each interdisciplinary sub-corpus. As explained by Biber (1995), every linguistic feature shows a certain degree of variability across the texts of a corpus. Thus a linguistic feature can be relatively common in some texts but relatively rare in others. The variance of the distribution of the studied features serves to measure how dispersed those values are across the total range of variation. In other words, it is important to examine whether "most values are closer to the mean value" (with only a few texts whose values are nearer the minimum and maximum), or whether "the values are more widely scattered" (with many texts whose values are nearer the minimum and maximum) (Biber, 1995, p. 109). By paying attention to the range and dispersion of the citations across the individual papers of each interdisciplinary sub-corpus, we have a clearer picture of how uniform the distribution of the features across the articles is. Therefore, it is clear that if the distribution of the linguistic features is not relatively uniform across the texts, the validity of the results obtained might be challenged. In order to examine the possible influence of these aspects, a boxplot diagram showing such distribution has been presented in Section 3.1.2. Again, the issue of variation across individual texts has been already considered in cross-disciplinary previous research, and this is why such analysis was not applied to the monodisciplinary sub-corpora in this study.

2.2.3 Identification of Citations

Citations can be expressed differently according to the style conventions of each journal. Different types of guidelines are used in the journals that make up the corpus: the American Psychological Association Style (APA), the Harvard or author-date system, the Chicago Manual of Style (CMOS), and the Council of Sciences Editors (CSE).

In the journals from neuroscience (*Neuroscience*), education (*International Journal of Educational Research*), and economics (*Quarterly Journal of Economics*), as well as in one of the Educational Neuroscience journals (*Mind, Brain, & Education*) and in one of the Economic History journals (*Journal of Economic History*), citations follow the APA and Harvard guidelines, which basically consist of the surname(s) of the author(s) followed by the year of publication, as in the examples that follow:

(1)   Nonetheless, Hacker, Hilde, and Jones (2010, p. 49) find little evidence of a "marriage squeeze" for women, noting that, instead of forgoing marriage entirely, women may have "relaxed their standards of acceptable partners." [EH]

(2)   In recent years, motilin has been considered as a new treatment modality (Chapman et al., 2013). [NEU]

The CSE guidelines are used in one of the Educational Neuroscience journals (*Trends in Neuroscience and Education*) as well as in the journals from biomedicine (*Biology and Medicine Journal*) and computer engineering (*International Journal of Advanced Research in Computer Engineering & Technology*). According to this system, citations are expressed through indicating references by number(s) in square brackets in line with the text. The actual authors can be referred to, but the reference number(s) must always be given, as in the following examples:

(3)   The formation of new capillaries also took place at this phase, which began when there was in ammation [12,13]. [BIO]

(4)   For example, Seger et al. [64] tracked neural response patterns as individuals became more proficient at classifying instances into categories. [EN]

Finally, the CMOS offers two different systems. One is the *notes and bibliography* system, according to which sources are cited in numbered footnotes or endnotes, where each note corresponds to a raised (superscript) number in the text. The other is the *author–date* system, according to which sources are briefly cited in the text, usually in parentheses, by author's last name and year of publication, which is similar to APA or Harvard style. For example, in one of the journals from Science and Technology Studies (*Science, Technology, & Human Values*) the CMOS author–date system is used, while in the other (*Science and Engineering Ethics*), both CMOS systems are permitted. In the journals from ethics (*Ethics*), history (*Journal of Contemporary History*), and one of the journals from Economic History (*Economic History Review*), however, only the CMOS notes and bibliography system is used, as exemplified below:

(5)   Like Barker, Kay argues that business ownership continued to be a "useful and possible avenue for women".[8] [EH]

(6)   As a consequence, historians have focused almost exclusively on the most visible, most abrasive German campaign of the early 1920s in order to [...].[7] [HIS]

Due to the variety of citation styles employed, the search and identification of citations was not an easy task, especially in the history, ethics, Economic History, and one of the Science and Technology Studies sub-corpora, since footnotes or endnotes did not always refer to references but also to different comments or clarifications. As a result, although footnotes and endnotes had been removed from the articles when preparing them for storage as .txt files, those that referred to external references in these sub-corpora were restored for matters of identification.

In order to cover all instances of citations, the corpus was computer-searched for numerous features (Hyland, 2000), such as dates between parentheses, numbers in square brackets, superscript numbers, quotation marks, and references to other citations (for example, *op cit.*, *ibid.*, etc.). Furthermore, concordance searches were made with the surnames listed in the references for confirmation (before they were removed from the corpus), and third person pronouns and phrases such as *these researchers* or *these authors* were also searched. However, instances of self-citation were excluded following Hyland (2000) and Petrić (2012).

3 Comparison between Interdisciplinary and Monodisciplinary Writing: Visibility and Strength of External Sources

The main aim of this section is to compare the monodisciplinary sub-corpora from each set with the corresponding interdisciplinary ones. In order to do this, the citations in the Educational Neuroscience articles are analyzed in comparison with the neuroscience and education ones; the Economic History articles are compared with the economics and history ones; and the articles from the Science and Technology Studies journals are compared with those from ethics, biomedicine, and computer engineering.

Three main aspects are analyzed in turn. First, the issue of citation density is considered so as to explore the hypothesis that, as citations are more varied in interdisciplinary writing, they will be more frequent than in monodisciplinary writing. Second, the visibility and, third, the strength of external sources in each sub-corpus are investigated to test the hypothesis that citation practices that are typical of the single-domain disciplines will also be present in the interdisciplinary journals.

By distinguishing between integral and nonintegral citations, the degree of visibility of the projecting sources is explored, which allows us to determine the extent to which external sources are foregrounded or backgrounded in the discourse (Hood, 2011). Furthermore, the difference between attributed and averred sources helps to determine a cline of propositional responsibility (Groom, 2000) between both poles, which, in turn, makes the external author's voice stronger or weaker. Variation in the degrees of both visibility and strength of external sources are common linguistic devices used in academic writing across disciplines. By studying such phenomena throughout the corpus, the first research question on the extent to which citation practices in the interdisciplines are drawn from those in the single-domain disciplines is addressed. At the end of this section, an attempt is made at contextualizing the findings obtained in the light of contrasting types of interdisciplinarity (Klein, 2017) that are framed by epistemological considerations.

3.1 Frequency of Citations

Every occurring citation was identified in the 450 complete RAs that make up the whole corpus. Then, citations were counted and citation density rates were calculated for each sub-corpus. After that, the issues of variation across interdisciplinary journals from the same field and variation across the individual articles from each interdisciplinary sub-corpus were examined.

In this first stage of the analysis, a total of 21,636 citations were identified in the whole corpus, and citation density rates per 1,000 words were calculated for every sub-corpus. In the case of the sub-corpus of Science and Technology Studies, RAs were grouped according to the two topics selected (bioethics and engineering ethics). It is important to make clear that both topics are covered in both Science and Technology Studies journals. Thus, in order to keep a balance, thirteen texts from one journal and twelve texts from the other journal were grouped to make up one topical sub-corpus (bioethics), while twelve texts from the first journal and thirteen texts from the second journal were put together to make up the second topical sub-corpus (engineering ethics). Results are presented in Tables 3.1, 3.2, and 3.3:

Table 3.1 Citation density in Set 1: neuroscience, education, and Educational Neuroscience

SET 1	Number of words	Citation tokens	Citation density (per 1,000 words)
Neuroscience	232,092	2,593	11.17
Education	318,513	2,853	8.95
Educational Neuroscience	275,466	3,149	11.43

Table 3.2 Citation density in Set 2: economics, history, and Economic History

SET 2	Number of words	Citation tokens	Citation density (per 1,000 words)
Economics	607,852	1,893	3.11
History	462,631	3,380	7.30
Economic History	416,062	3,159	7.59

Table 3.3 Citation density in Set 3: ethics, biomedicine, computer engineering, and Science and Technology Studies

SET 3	Number of words	Citation tokens	Citation density (per 1,000 words)
Ethics	549,235	1,750	3.18
Biomedicine	48,336	432	8.93
Computer engineering	59,017	299	5.06
Biomedicine and computer engineering	107,353	731	6.8
STS Topic 1: bioethics	149,542	1,138	7.6
STS Topic 2: engineering ethics	190,461	990	5.19
Science and Technology Studies	340,003	2,128	6.25

These tables show that the frequency of citations varies between disciplines in the three sets studied. In order to explain this variation, it is necessary first to provide some parameters of comparison between the rates found in this study for the single-domain disciplines and the rates found by other researchers in similar disciplines. For example, in one of the most cited studies on disciplinary variation, Hyland (2000) calculated rates per 1,000 words from 10.1 to 12.5 in social science texts, which could be compared with the rate for education (8.95) and economics (3.11) in this study. Findings here are rather different from Hyland's: the citation rate is slightly lower for education but even more markedly lower for economics. However, Thompson (2001) found a citation density rate of 6.7 per 1,000 words in his corpus of agricultural economics articles and of 5.25 per 1,000 words in his corpus of agricultural economics PhD theses, thus also showing disagreement with the rates calculated by Hyland (2000) for other social sciences. Thompson (2005) suggests that this could be a specific feature of writing in the discipline of economics. The lower citation density rate calculated for economics in this study might provide evidence for the same argument. Similarly, Fløttum et. al. (2006) also calculated a citation density rate of 3.96 in a corpus of economics RAs.

As regards frequency of citations in the natural sciences and technologies, exemplified in this corpus by neuroscience, biomedicine, and computer engineering articles, similar figures to those reported by other researchers were encountered. A citation density rate of 11.17 per 1,000 words was calculated for articles in neuroscience, followed by 8.93 in the articles from biomedicine and 5.06 in those from computer engineering. Hyland's (2000) rate for biology was 15.15 citations per 1,000 words, while Thompson (2005) reported a rate of 9.0 citations per 1,000 words in his agricultural botany corpus. Thus the rate calculated in this study would be between these, although nearer Thompson's (2005) figure. As for biomedicine articles, which reported a density rate of 8.93 citations per 1,000 words, it is to be highlighted that Hyland's (2000) rate for biology is again higher when compared. However, a study by Hu and Wang (2014) reported a citation density rate of 8.75 per 1,000 words in general medicine articles, thus showing a clear similarity with the findings in this study. Finally, Hyland (2000) reported a rate of between 7.3 and 8.4 citations per 1,000 words for two branches of engineering, which is, again, higher than the 5.06 rate calculated in this study for computer engineering articles.

As for humanities, a citation density rate of 7.30 citations per 1,000 words was calculated for history articles, while 3.18 citations per 1,000 words were counted in ethics articles. While the rate for history is similar to that calculated by Hyland (2000) for philosophy (10.8), another humanity, the lower rate calculated for ethics would need additional explanations that might be offered if a more thorough study of this discipline in particular is carried out. To my knowledge, no citation studies on the field of ethics have been published for comparison purposes.

Focusing now on the comparison between each interdiscipline with the two related disciplines in each set, some useful findings can be reported. The citation density rate for Educational Neuroscience articles is 11.43, which is higher than both education (8.95) and neuroscience (11.17) texts. In a similar vein, the frequency of citations for Economic History is 7.59 per 1,000 words, which is higher than both economics (3.11) and history (7.30). The same trend is observed when the citation rate of 5.19 for Science and Technology Studies articles dealing with topic 2 (engineering ethics) is compared with the rates in ethics (3.18) and computer engineering (5.06) respectively. However, the calculated citation rate of 7.6 for articles that deal with topic 1 (bioethics) is lower when compared with the rate for biomedicine (8.93), although the higher frequency of citations that occurs in biology articles in particular has been specifically highlighted by Hyland (2000) and Swales (2014) as a typicality of the discipline. Despite this single discrepancy, the findings obtained provide preliminary evidence for similar or even higher citation frequencies in the interdisciplines when compared with their related single-domain disciplines in the three cases. By means of the web-based calculator developed by the Lancaster UCREL site[7], log-likelihood (LL) values have been calculated to test the significance of the findings obtained as regards the differences in citation density rates between the interdisciplines and each constituent monodiscipline in the three sets. The results are shown in Table 3.4.

---

[7] http://ucrel.lancs.ac.uk/llwizard

Table 3.4 Log-likelihood values for citations density rates in monodisciplinary vs. interdisciplinary articles

	Citation density (per 1,000 words)		Citation density (per 1,000 words)	Log-likelihood value
SET 1				
Neuroscience	11.17	Educational Neuroscience	11.43	0.75
Education	8.95	Educational Neuroscience	11.43	**89.19**
SET 2				
Economics	3.11	Economic History	7.59	**981.03**
History	7.30	Economic History	7.59	2.42
SET 3				
Ethics	3.18	Science and Technology Studies	6.25	**439.05**
Biomedicine and comp. eng.	6.80	Science and Technology Studies	6.25	3.81

In order to understand these kinds of findings, Rayson (2017) provides references to interpret LL values in terms of probability (p) terms, as illustrated in Table 3.5.

Table 3.5 Log-likelihood reference values

LL value ranges	Significance values (p)	Degree of certainty
3.84–6.62	0.05	95%
6.63–10.82	0.01	99%
10.83–15.12	0.001	99.90%
>15.13	0.0001	99.99%

For example, if the log-likelihood value is greater than 6.63, the probability of the result happening by chance is less than 1 percent. This is usually expressed as $p < 0.01$. If the log-likelihood value is 3.84 or more, the probability of it happening by chance is less than 5 percent and this is expressed as $p < 0.05$ (Rayson, 2017).

From the log-likelihood values calculated in this study, it can be inferred that the hypothesis that citations are more frequent in interdisciplinary writing when compared with monodisciplinary articles is only true in the following three cases, where the differences in citation density rates are statistically significant: (1) when Educational Neuroscience is compared with education (LL = 89.19); (2) when Economic History is compared with economics (LL = 981.03); and (3) when Science and Technology Studies is compared with ethics (LL = 439.05). In the other three cases, however, as calculated LL values represent p values that are <0.05, the hypothesis cannot be completely accepted, since there is less than 95 percent confidence that the observed differences have arisen by chance (McEnery et al., 2006).

To sum up, this first stage was aimed at finding out whether citations are similarly or even more frequent in the interdisciplinary fields when compared with the single-domain disciplines. Although at first sight this hypothesis might be proved right, further tests carried out showed that differences of rates between the interdisciplines and their constituent monodisciplines were only statistically significant for three out of the six cases evaluated. Thus further more authoritative studies need to be carried out in order to test such hypotheses.

3.1.1 Citation Density: Variation across Journals from the Same Interdisciplines

A comparison between the journals from each interdiscipline was carried out so as to prevent possible problems of local densities (Moon, 1998). In order to explore this issue, citation density rates were calculated for the interdisciplinary journals' sub-corpora. The results are reported in Table 3.6.

Table 3.6 Comparison of citation density rates in different journals from each interdiscipline

	Number of words	Citation tokens	Citation density (per 1,000 words)
Educational Neuroscience journals			
Trends in Neuroscience and Education	143,995	1,784	12.39
Mind, Brain, & Education	131,471	1,365	10.38
Economic History journals			
Journal of Economic History	208,415	1,450	6.95
Economic History Review	207,647	1,709	8.23

Table 3.6 (cont.)

	Number of words	Citation tokens	Citation density (per 1,000 words)
Science and Technology Studies journals			
Science and Engineering Ethics	171,688	1,038	6.04
Science, Technology, & Human Values	168,315	1,090	6.47

According to the findings, citations show similar normalized frequencies in both journals from the same interdisciplines. This similarity is most marked in the two journals from Science and Technology Studies, where a citation density rate of 6.04 was found in *Science and Engineering Ethics* and a rate of 6.47 was calculated in *Science, Technology, & Human Values*. In the journals from Economic History, the variation between journals is very low. While a rate of 6.95 citations per 1,000 words was found for the *Journal of Economic History*, in the *Economic History Review* the rate was 8.23. As for Educational Neuroscience, a higher normalized frequency of 12.39 citations per 1,000 words was encountered in *Trends in Neuroscience and Education* when compared with *Mind, Brain, & Education* (10.38). As a whole, it might be concluded that there is a certain homogeneity between the two journals from each interdiscipline as regards citation density. In order to test the significance of such differences, log-likelihood values have been calculated. The results are shown in Table 3.7.

Table 3.7 Log-likelihood values for citations density rates in different journals from each interdiscipline

	Citation density (per 1,000 words)		Citation density (per 1,000 words)	Log-likelihood value
Educational Neuroscience journals				
Trends in Neuroscience and Education	12.39	*Mind, Brain, & Education*	10.38	**24.31**

Table 3.7 (cont.)

	Citation density (per 1,000 words)		Citation density (per 1,000 words)	Log-likelihood value
Economic History journals				
Journal of Economic History	6.95	*Economic History Review*	8.23	**22.23**
Science and Technology Studies journals				
Science and Engineering Ethics	6.04	*Science, Techno, -logy& Human Values*	6.47	**2.51**

From the log-likelihood values calculated, it can be inferred that the expected degree of homogeneity in citation density rates between different journals from the same interdisciplinary field is only supported in the case of the Educational Neuroscience journals (LL = 24.31) and Economic History ones (LL = 22.23). In the case of Science and Technology Studies, however, as the LL value represents a *p* value which is <0.05 (LL = 2.51), the idea that there is a certain homogeneity as regards the number of citations counted in the two different journals from the same interdiscipline cannot be completely accepted, since there is less than 95 percent confidence that the observed difference has arisen by chance (McEnery et al., 2006).

3.1.2 Citation Density: Variation across Individual Articles from Interdisciplinary Journals

The next step was to consider the issue of range and dispersion of the linguistic features across individual papers in the interdisciplinary sub-corpora. The findings obtained are shown in Figure 3.1.

Findings show that the three sub-corpora are more or less uniform as regards the range and dispersion of the frequencies of citations normalized per 1,000 words in each individual article. Nevertheless, some issues need to be acknowledged. First, the citations in the Educational Neuroscience corpus are more widely dispersed than

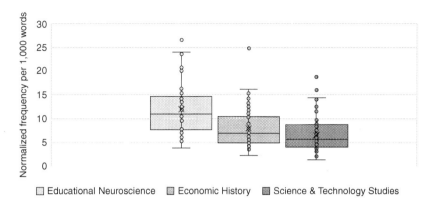

Figure 3.1 Range and dispersion of citations in individual articles in the three interdisciplines

in the other two corpora. In other words, the Economic History and Science and Technology Studies texts are more uniform as regards the distribution of citations. Second, there are a few cases in the three sets that stand out and that are displayed outside the scope of the whiskers as separate data points that constitute outliers. However, as they are represented by only 4 texts out of 150, it is likely that the results obtained have not been markedly skewed.

So far, citations have been identified and citation density rates have been calculated for the articles in the whole corpus. Furthermore, the issues of variation across interdisciplinary journals from the same field as well as variation across the individual articles from each interdisciplinary sub-corpus have been considered. In the following sections, two analytical dimensions will be considered: the degrees of visibility and the strength of the external sources.

3.2 Visibility of External Sources: Integral vs. Nonintegral Citations

According to Hood (2011, p. 111), there are "significant differences in how projecting voices are represented" in discourse. Hood (2011) refers to the degree of visibility of sources based on the concept of *projection* introduced by Halliday and Matthiessen: "[t]hrough projection one clause is set up as the representation of the linguistic 'content' of another" (Halliday and Matthiessen, 2004, p. 443). In this regard, citation conventions, as well as choices related to whether to include the writer's name within the flow of the discourse or not, play an important role. Some referencing conventions, as already acknowledged, indicate that the author's sur-name must appear in the flow of the text, whether in an integral or a nonintegral way. An integral citation is one "in which the name of the researcher occurs in the actual citing sentence as some sentence-element"; in a nonintegral citation, the researcher occurs "either in parenthesis or is referred to elsewhere by a superscript number or via some other device" (Swales, 1990, p. 148). In nonintegral citations, the cited source is less visible than in an integral citation. Thus citation conventions and types of citations are linguistic resources that serve to show the degree of visibility of the projecting sources and the extent to which they are "foregrounded" or "backgrounded" in the discourse (Hood, 2011, p. 111). In similar terms, integral citations are sometimes referred to as "author prominent," while nonintegral citations are called "research prominent" (Feak and Swales, 2009, p. 45).

Examples (7), (8), and (9) from articles with different style conventions are all cases of integral citations, which include the cited author(s) within the grammar of the sentence, thus giving prominence to the messenger.

(7)   Our data provided further empirical evidence for the three sources of vulnerability, as defined by <u>Kelchtermans (2009, 2011)</u>: teachers' inability to control essential working conditions, difficulty to prove one's effectiveness as a teacher, and the inevitable uncertainty in their judging and decision-making. [EDU]

(8)   A recent study by <u>Christakou et al. [5] investigated</u> the neural maturation that accompanies this. They found that the previously observed age-related decrease in impulsive choices during adolescence was associated with changes in activation in the limbic corticostriatal network in the brain [. . .]. [EN]

(9)   <u>Lucía Prieto Borrego and Encarnación Barranquero Texeira</u>, who have examined the Republican authorities' establishment of "popular tribunals" in Malaga, similarly acknowledge that some of the new groups [. . .] "enjoyed a measure of institutional support and a number of them even played a role in the government court system".<u>[21]</u> [HIS]

In contrast, nonintegral citations refer to sources in parentheses, square brackets, or superscript numbers, where the emphasis is placed on the reported message, as in examples (10), (11), and (12).

(10)   In a previous study, it is found that the motilin receptor agonist erythromycin can significantly inhibit the mouse hippocampal neurons <u>(Lu et al., 2009)</u>. [NEU]

(11)   Heat stroke is also an ancient illness dating back more than two thousand years and its pathology has been attributed to the effects of hyperthermia and heat toxicity <u>[3–5]</u>. [BIO]

(12)   In particular, some authors depart only partially from the established idea that female-owned businesses were not only smaller than male-owned ones but also traded in [. . .].<u>[10]</u> [EH]

Hood (2011, p. 115) posits that the different representations of projecting sources can be "plotted along a continuum." The invisible voice, where the cited researcher is omitted from the flow of discourse and referenced only by means of a super- or subscript number, more typical of the natural sciences, would be placed at one extreme. Those voices made integral to the flow of discourse – which are copresent in time and place with what is observed; more typical of the humanities – would be placed at the other extreme. The voices in the social sciences, however, "would occupy middle ground between the natural sciences and the humanities" (Hood, 2011, p. 118). That is, if placed within the continuum, such voices are made less visible than those from the humanities but more visible than those from the natural sciences.

Following the above considerations, citations were classified according to the distinctions of both types into integral and nonintegral citations. The findings obtained for each disciplinary set have been summarized in Tables 3.8, 3.9, 3.10, and 3.11. They have also been illustrated in Figures 3.2, 3.3, 3.4, and 3.5 respectively:

Table 3.8 Frequency of integral/nonintegral citations in Set 1: neuroscience, education, and Educational Neuroscience

SET 1	Integral citations	Nonintegral citations	Total citations
Neuroscience	152 (5.80%)	2,441 (94.20%)	2,593 (100%)
Education	817 (28.63%)	2,036 (71.37%)	2,853 (100%)
Educational Neuroscience	466 (18.17%)	2,683 (81.83%)	3,149 (100%)

SET 1: Integral vs. nonintegral citations

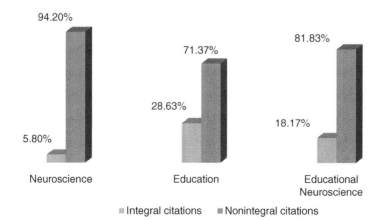

Figure 3.2 Percentage of integral/nonintegral citations in Set 1: neuroscience, education, and Educational Neuroscience

Table 3.9 Frequency of integral/nonintegral citations in Set 2: economics, history, and Economic History

SET 2	Integral citations	Nonintegral citations	Total citations
Economics	1,150 (60.75%)	743 (39.25%)	1,893 (100%)
History	935 (27.67%)	2,445 (72.33%)	3,380 (100%)
Economic History	975 (30.86%)	2,184 (69.14%)	3,159 (100%)

Table 3.10 Frequency of integral/nonintegral citations in Set 3 (Topic 1): ethics, biomedicine, and Science and Technology Studies

SET 3 (Topic 1)	Integral citations	Nonintegral citations	Total citations
Ethics	976 (55.77%)	774 (44.23%)	1,750 (100%)
Biomedicine	65 (15.04%)	367 (84.96%)	432 (100%)
STS (bioethics)	200 (17.57%)	938 (82.43%)	1,138 (100%)

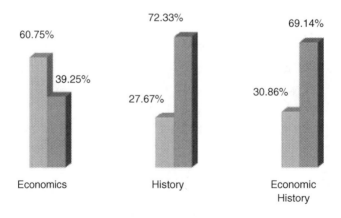

SET 2: Integral vs. nonintegral citations

Integral citations   Nonintegral citations

Figure 3.3 Percentage of integral/nonintegral citations in Set 2: economics, history, and Economic History

Table 3.11 Frequency of integral/nonintegral citations in Set 3 (Topic 2): ethics, computer engineering, and Science and Technology Studies

SET 3 (Topic 2)	Integral citations	Nonintegral citations	Total citations
Ethics	976 (55.77%)	774 (44.23%)	1,750 (100%)
Computer engineering	82 (27.42%)	217 (72.58%)	299 (100%)
STS (engineering ethics)	321 (32.43%)	669 (67.57%)	990 (100%)

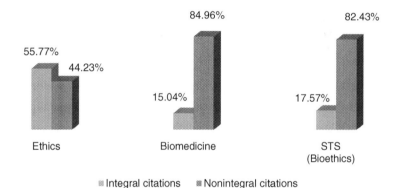

SET 3 (Topic 1): Integral vs. nonintegral citations

Figure 3.4 Percentage of integral/nonintegral citations in Set 3 (Topic 1): ethics, biomedicine, and Science and Technology Studies

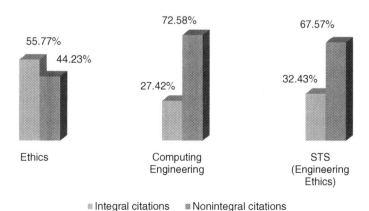

SET 3 (Topic 2): Integral vs. nonintegral citations

Figure 3.5 Percentage of integral/nonintegral citations in Set 3 (Topic 2): ethics, computer engineering, and Science and Technology Studies

The first conclusion derived from these findings is that the frequency of integral and nonintegral citations in the single-domain disciplines is mostly concurrent with previous research. It has been acknowledged that, although both *hard* and *soft* sciences (as referred to by Hyland, 2000) use more nonintegral than integral references, there is a greater proportion of integral references in the soft sciences when compared with the hard sciences. In this corpus too, it can be observed that the frequency of integral citations is lower in neuroscience, biomedicine, and engineering than in the other disciplines. The only exception in Hyland's (2000) study was philosophy, a humanity, where the frequency of integral citations was higher than that of nonintegral ones. Interestingly, a similar trend is observed in this corpus for ethics, which is, in fact, a branch of philosophy.

Some discrepancies are observed in the fields of economics and history. In economics, which is a social science, the frequency of integral references (60.75%) is higher than in history (39.25%), which is a humanity, thereby contradicting not only Hyland's (2000) conclusions but also Hood's (2011) understanding of the existence of a continuum that goes from the least visible end (natural sciences) to the most visible end (humanities) when locating projected sources according to their degree of visibility. However, these findings concur with Thompson and Tribble (2001, p. 94), who reported that 61.9 percent of citations were integral and 38.1 percent were nonintegral in their corpus of agricultural economics PhD theses. Although there is a difference as regards genre, the coincidence is worth mentioning for the purpose of this study. As for the lower frequency of integral references in history articles in this corpus, a plausible explanation is that, as pointed out by Bondi (2015, p. 163), the "basically narrative structure of historical discourse may **reduce the visibility** of argument" (emphasis is mine). As historians present an interpretation of historical facts, "they do so by bringing in relevant facts and relevant sources and by showing how these facts and sources support their own interpretation" (Bondi, 2015, p. 153). In other words, if there is an emphasis on self-interpretation rather than on attribution to others, those others are brought into the text in less visible ways; that is, by means of nonintegral references. Furthermore, Coffin (2009) adds that this is particularly the case when footnotes are used for referencing, as in the articles from the history corpus in this study.

3.2.1 Visibility: Comparison of Interdisciplines and Monodisciplines

Moving now to a comparison of interdisciplines with their related single-domain disciplines, the findings show that in all three cases the frequencies of integral and nonintegral citations are between the inter- and single-discipline numbers. However, despite this similarity, there are important differences between the sets.

In Set 1, the differences between the percentages of integral and nonintegral citations across neuroscience, education, and Educational Neuroscience are similar, although the difference between the interdiscipline and education (around 10%) is slightly lower when compared with neuroscience (around 12%). This suggests a greater influence of education over the interdiscipline. In Set 2, however, the difference is much higher when the percentage of integral and nonintegral citations in Economic History is compared with economics (around 30%) than when compared with history (around 3%). In this case, a clearer resemblance between history and Economic History articles can be observed, thereby showing a greater influence of the humanity. Similarly, in Set 3, the percentages of integral and nonintegral citations in Science and Technology Studies stand in the middle between ethics and biomedicine, and ethics and computer engineering, respectively. Again, the difference is much higher when compared with ethics, which is around 40% in the case of Topic 1 (bioethics) and around 20% in the case of Topic 2 (engineering ethics), than when compared with biomedicine (around 2.5%) and computer engineering (around 5%) respectively. It is clear, then, that Science and Technology Studies articles are more similar to biomedicine and computer engineering articles than to ethics ones, thus showing a greater influence from the natural sciences and technologies.

As a preliminary conclusion, it can be acknowledged that as regards the degree of visibility of external sources according to the frequency of integral and nonintegral citations, there is a tendency for interdisciplinary writing to be located in the middle of the two monodisciplinary fields. Yet the differences encountered between a more or less marked influence from each single-domain discipline deserve special attention. These will be treated at the end, in Section 3.4, together with the conclusions from the analysis of averred and attributed sources discussed below in Section 3.3.

3.3 Strength of External Sources: Attributed vs. Averred Citations

Averral and attribution are basic notions for the organization of interaction in a written text (Tadros, 1993). As put by Hunston (2004, p. 16, following Sinclair, 1988), "an attributed statement is essentially one that is said to belong to someone other than the current writer," while an averred statement "is made by the current writer." Thus averral is the "default condition" of a written text (Tadros, 1993, p. 101) since "it identifies, and is thus identified with, the textual voice of the writer herself or himself." Attribution, as stated by Thompson

(2012, p. 121) is "the use of manifest intertextual markers (usually citations) to acknowledge an antecedent authorial voice." According to Hunston (2004, p. 19) attribution is the way in which "voices other than the writer's are brought into a text and manipulated by the writer." Finally, although attribution and averral are in a certain sense oppositional, it is the interplay of both that allows the writer to gain position (Hunston, 2000).

Considering that "attribution involves both the writer's voice and that of the attributee," Hunston (2011, p. 38) argues that "the **writer's voice** is **stronger** where the attribution **is not** expressed through a *that*-clause" (emphasis is mine) (Hunston, 2011, p. 38). As a conclusion derived from this assertion, we can also say that it is the **external author's voice** that is **stronger** where the attribution **is** expressed through a *that*-clause. Consequently, the external author's voice becomes less strong when other markers of attribution are used (for example *according to*, *as*, *for*, etc.) and even weaker in cases in which citations are part of averred statements. When I refer to *strength* as a parameter of analysis, I am referring thus to the strength of the cited author's voice, which is stronger in a citation that introduces an attributed proposition and weaker in a citation that is embedded in an averred statement. The concept of attribution is also commonly used to refer to the responsibility for a proposition (Thompson, 2005). For example, Groom (2000) claims that there exists "a cline of propositional responsibility" between the poles of averral and attribution. In this way, when there is attribution, the attributed author's voice is stronger because he or she is also given the responsibility for the proposition.

Examples (13), (14), (15), and (16) show all cases of *attribution through citation*, since in all them a proposition has been attributed to an external source:

(13)   Reifel (1984) suggests that blocks allow children to play directly with spatial concepts, which in turn could assist their developing representations [. . .]. [EN]

(14)   As pointed out by LaFallotte (2007), moral habits are of critical importance [. . .]. [STS]

(15)   According to historian Vijay Prashad, this cooperation aimed to work against what many delegates viewed as the "indignity of imperialism's cultural chauvinism".[46] [HIS]

(16)   [. . .] and for Damico, Campano and Harste (2009, p. 175), 'a proliferation of meanings, rather than single or fixed meanings, could become a standard approach to literacy interpretation or textual response'. [EDU]

As for *averral through citation*, or *averred sources*, the examples below show different cases. For instance, in example (17), "while the evidence for the truth value of the statement is attributed to the other, the voice of the text is that of the writer" (Thompson, 2005, p. 36), since it is the writer who has interpreted the propositions. This phenomenon has been also called "sourced averral" (Hunston, 2000, p. 192), and its use is meant basically to acknowledge the identification of the external source:

(17)   Allopregnanolone is one of the most potent and efficacious positive allosteric modulators of GABA receptor function (Majewska, 1992; Lambert et al., 1995), and its administration induces marked anxiolytic effects in animals (Majewska, 1992; Bitran et al., 1995). [NEU]

In example (18), the citation is attached to "a summary or interpretation of what other researchers found" (Thompson, 2005, p. 37) and it is clear that the cited authors are not responsible for the proposition because it is the writer who is responsible for the summary:

(18)   There are several studies that examine the role of human capital in context of the Industrial Revolution since the seminal work of David Mitch (1999, 2004) and Lars G. Sandberg (1979) showed the relative unimportance of traditionally measured human capital (i.e., formal schooling and literacy). [EH]

There are other cases in which the source of the citation is accompanied by a reporting verb that describes a research process, as in example (19). In these cases, there is a summary or retelling of what the other authors did, and, again, it is the current writer who is responsible for that summary or interpretation:

(19)   Authors in [6] used CNN with pre trained models. Authors in [7][8] used 3d CNN rather 2d CNN to detect Alzheimer's disease. Authors in [9] used CNN architecture to brain identified graph detected from MRI DTI (diffusion tensor imaging). [ENG]

Following these considerations for the identification of attributed or averred sources, every citation was classified accordingly into cases of attribution through citations (without differentiating between different grammatical structures) or averral through citations (without differentiating between different types). The findings obtained for each disciplinary set have been summarized in Tables 3.12, 3.13, 3.14, and 3.15. They have been also illustrated by Figures 3.6, 3.7, 3.8, and 3.9.

Table 3.12 Frequency of averred/attributed citations in Set 1: neuroscience, education, and Educational Neuroscience

SET 1	Averred citations	Attributed citations	Total citations
Neuroscience	2,127 (82.03%)	466 (17.97%)	2,593 (100%)
Education	2,467 (86.47%)	386 (13.53%)	2,853 (100%)
Educational Neuroscience	2,701 (85.78%)	448 (14.22%)	3,149 (100%)

Table 3.13 Frequency of averred/attributed citations in Set 2: economics, history, and Economic History

SET 2	Averred citations	Attributed citations	Total citations
Economics	1,640 (86.64%)	253 (13.36%)	1,893 (100%)
History	2,040 (60.35%)	1,340 (39.65%)	3,380 (100%)
Economic History	2,623 (83.03%)	536 (16.97%)	3,159 (100%)

SET 1: Averred vs. attributed citations

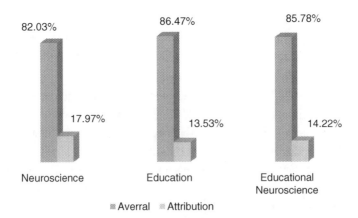

Figure 3.6 Percentage of averred/attributed citations in Set 1: neuroscience, education, and Educational Neuroscience

Table 3.14 Frequency of averred/attributed citations in Set 3 (Topic 1): ethics, biomedicine, and Science and Technology Studies

SET 3 (Topic 1)	Averred citations	Attributed citations	Total citations
Ethics	979 (55.95%)	771 (44.05%)	1,750 (100%)
Biomedicine	342 (79.17%)	90 (20.83%)	432 (100%)
STS (bioethics)	855 (75.13%)	283 (24.87%)	1,138 (100%)

Table 3.15 Frequency of averred/attributed citations in Set 3 (Topic 2): ethics, computer engineering, and Science and Technology Studies

SET 3 (Topic 2)	Averred citations	Attributed citations	Total citations
Ethics	979 (55.95%)	771 (44.05%)	1,750 (100%)
Computer engineering	266 (88.97%)	33 (11.03%)	299 (100%)
STS (engineering ethics)	692 (69.90%)	298 (30.10%)	990 (100%)

SET 2: Averred vs. attributed citations

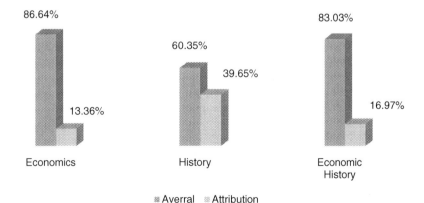

Figure 3.7 Percentage of averred/attributed citations in Set 2: economics, history, and Economic History

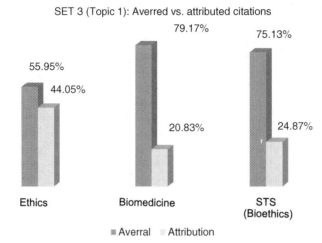

Figure 3.8 Percentage of averred/attributed citations in Set 3 (Topic 1): ethics, biomedicine, and Science and Technology Studies

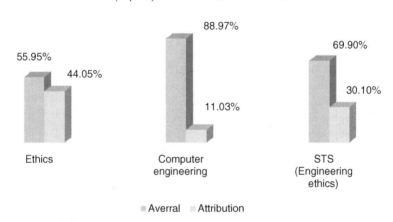

Figure 3.9 Percentage of averred/attributed4 citations in Set 3 (Topic 2): ethics, computer engineering, and Science and Technology Studies

No previous research on the frequency of averred and attributed sources in academic disciplines, to my knowledge, has been carried out in order to provide some parameters of comparison with the frequencies encountered for the single-domain disciplines in this study. However, some preliminary conclusions can be presented from the findings obtained. First, it is clear that cases of averral through citation are more frequent than cases of attribution through citations in all the disciplines. Second, it might seem that the humanities, represented here by ethics (44.05%) and history (39.65%), show a clear preference for conveying attribution when compared with the natural sciences, represented here by neuroscience (17.97%), biomedicine (20.83%), and computer engineering (11.03%), as well as when compared with the social sciences, represented here by economics (13.36%) and education (13.53%). This means that, although there is a general preference in all the disciplines for using citations in which the current writer has the responsibility for the proposition, and therefore has a stronger voice in comparison with that of the cited author, this tendency is less marked in the humanities. Thus, because of the higher percentages of attributed sources in comparison with the other disciplines, external voices are made stronger and they are given more responsibility for the cited propositions in humanities disciplines.

3.3.1 Strength: Comparison of Interdisciplines and Monodisciplines

Considering now the frequency of attributed and averred sources in the three interdisciplines when compared with their related disciplines, results indicate that, similarly to what was observed for the parameter of visibility, the percentages of attributed and averred sources stand in the middle when compared with the single-domain disciplines in the three disciplinary sets. However, those differences are more or less marked depending on the case.

As regards Set 1, the differences between the percentages of attributed and averred sources across the three fields are minimal, although the difference between Educational Neuroscience and education (around 1%) is lower when compared with neuroscience (around 4%), thus showing a slightly greater influence from education over the interdiscipline, as observed from the analysis of the visibility of sources. In the case of Set 2, the differences are more marked, and it is clear that the frequencies of attributed and averred citations are more similar between Economic History and economics, where the difference between percentages is lower (around 3%) in comparison with history (around 23%). This time, a greater influence from the social science than from the humanity is shown, contrary to what was observed when the visibility of the sources was analysed. As for the analysis of Set 3, the differences between the percentages are higher between ethics and Science and Technology Studies (16.50% on average from both sub-topics: 19.18% from bioethics and 13.95% from engineering ethics) than between Science and Technology Studies and biomedicine and computer engineering (around 11.50% on average from both fields: 6.66% from biomedicine and 16.46% from computer engineering). On this occasion, again, a greater influence from the natural sciences and technologies was observed, as occurred when the parameter of visibility was studied. It is important to notice, however, that this trend changes when journals from Topic 2 (engineering ethics) are considered in isolation in comparison with the sub-corpus from computer engineering. This time, the difference is greater between Science and Technology Studies and computer engineering (19.07%) when compared with ethics (13.95%). Further studies might be needed in order to reach more solid conclusions.

3.4 Preliminary Conclusions: Contrasting Types of Interdisciplinarity

Two different aspects of the analysis of citations have been explored in the three interdisciplines in comparison with the corresponding single-domain fields: the degree of visibility of the projecting sources and the degree of strength given to these voices. Findings show that, in the three cases and for the two aspects examined, the values calculated for the interdisciplinary fields stand in the middle between those of the relevant monodisciplines.

In their attempt to explore how interdisciplinary research fields create their own linguistic identities, Teich and Holtz (2009) examined the extent to which these fields make use of the existing linguistic conventions of the involved disciplines, whether by forming straight mergers, by creating new linguistic patterns, or by means of both. If the findings summarized above were interpreted in this way, it could be concluded that we are in the presence of truly merging disciplinary identities, at least as regards the citation aspects analyzed. However, such a statement would be an overgeneralization, considering that the degrees of influence from one or the other monodisciplines have been shown to differ in each set.

In order to provide some plausible interpretations that help us understand the different degrees of similarity and difference between the interdisciplines and the single-domain fields, the distinction of several contrasting types of interdisciplinarity (Klein, 2017) might prove useful. Moving from the more rigid concept of taxonomies adopted a decade ago (Klein, 2010) to a recent twist toward more adaptive and changing typologies, Klein (2017) attempts to describe different aspects of interdisciplinarity by exploring *contrasting typologies*. However, it is important to highlight that typologies are neither neutral nor static. They reflect "choices of representation in a semantic web of differing purposes, contexts, organizational structures, and epistemological frameworks" (Klein, 2017, p. 21). In this way, the aim of proposing such typologies is to extend, interrogate, or reformulate existing classifications so as to address different, new, and changing needs. As pointed out in the introduction, three types from different contrasting pairs have been selected to describe the interdisciplines and their related fields: *bridge-building* to refer to Educational

Neuroscience, *hybridization* as far as Economic History is concerned, and *critical* to describe Science and Technology Studies.

3.4.1 Educational Neuroscience: The Bridge-Building Type

In his seminal article "Education and the Brain: A Bridge Too Far," Bruer (1997) opened a debate arguing that the potential of neuroscience to directly influence education was limited. After twenty years, there are still those whose views are in line with such skepticism (e.g. Cuthbert, 2015; Bowers, 2016; Bruer, 2017; among others) and those who are more optimistic (Carew and Magsamen, 2010; Fischer et al., 2010; Gabrieli, 2016; among others). An issue shared by most, however, is the presence of the bridge metaphor and bridge-related titles, such as "build bridges" (e.g. Sigman et al., 2014; Willin, 2008), "envisioned bridges" (Baker et al., 2012), "boundaries as bridges" (Beauchamp and Beauchamp, 2013), and "bridges over troubled waters" (Ansari and Coch, 2006), among many others.

According to research focusing on the gap between neuroscience and education, several reasons are given for the difficulties in bridging the two fields. Among them, the presence of language barriers and poor communication between scientific researchers and educational practitioners (Pickering and Howard-Jones, 2007) are of most importance for the purpose of this study. According to education professionals (Edelenbosch et al., 2015), the way in which scientific articles are written makes it difficult for them to really engage with the results. Some others argued that neuroscientists make it hard for them to engage as equals by speaking in a language that excludes the participation of nonexperts. Most neuroscientists, however, mentioned that research findings need to be translated in order to be correctly interpreted by outsiders, and that translating this complex information without oversimplifying it was very difficult (Edelenbosch et al., 2015).

For the language aspects studied, namely the use of integral and nonintegral citations as well as the use of citations to convey attribution or averral, it can be concluded that Educational Neuroscience articles resemble education articles more than they do neuroscience ones. However, as already acknowledged, such a resemblance is not strongly marked. At first sight, it can be argued that as it is educators who have to make the greatest effort to understand the language of neuroscientists, which is usually aimed at experts only, citation practices reflect the disciplinary conventions of the former in what might be seen as an attempt to facilitate such understanding for nonexperts. In other words, by employing citation practices that are more common in education rather than in neuroscience articles, Educational Neuroscience writers in the corpus adopt practices that help to build a bridge towards the simplification of the scientists' language that is needed by the educational practitioners.

From another perspective, Schwartz et al. (2012) point out that in order to build a bridge between the two fields, it is important to distinguish two different but complementary Educational Neuroscience approaches. One is currently the dominant one, generally led by behavioral neuroscientists who find in education the topics and potential applications of their research. The less common second approach starts with educational researchers who look for behavioral neuroscientists to solve theoretical problems in education. In the first case, the initiators of the research are the neuroscientists, while in the second one, research is started by the educational researchers. Within the first approach, educators are seen as "implementers." In the light of the second, they are seen as "interpreters" (Schwartz et al., 2012, p. 9–10). Going back to the issue of language barriers, it can be claimed that depending on which approach is adopted, the language used would be more neuroscientist-friendly or more educator-friendly. In order to better understand the findings reported before, it might be useful to find out, in further studies, if the research carried out in the articles examined has been initiated by neuroscientists or by educational researchers (or both) and to explore their roles according to the approaches described. Furthermore, a more fine-grained analysis such as the one that will be carried out in Section 4 will help us to understand the gap and see why it is still so difficult to bridge it.

3.4.2 Economic History: The Hybrid Type

To Frickel (2004, p. 268), interdisciplines are "hybridized knowledge fields situated between and within existing disciplines." It has been already acknowledged that Economic History can be characterized as a hybrid. In fact, as Graff (2015b, p. 18) argues, the so-called "new histories" (new social, political, economic, cultural, racial, ethnic, and gender histories), which have developed on the borders of the humanities and the social sciences, have rarely found homes of their own. An exception has been Economic History, as Graff (2015b) points out. This seems to exemplify Klein's (2017, p. 22) point that some of these hybrids "develop epistemological strength anchored by shared thematic principles, unifying core concepts, and a common interlanguage."

This idea of a shared interlanguage might inform the understanding of the results obtained from the analysis of citations. On the one hand, Economic History articles resemble history ones as regards the use of integral and non-integral citations. On the other, they are more similar to economics articles as far as the presence of attributed and averred sources is concerned. Contrary to what was observed in the other two interdisciplines, where the influence of one of the disciplines was more noticeable for both linguistic aspects, in Economic History there is a clear notion of merging features in more or less similar ways from one and the other monodisciplines.

This somehow equal influence from both disciplines is also rooted in the fact that, as explained by Lamoreaux (2015, p.1251), most "economists and historians today accept the stereotype that economics is about generalization and history is about understanding specific phenomena in the past." However, efforts are also made by economic historians to operate somewhere in the middle of those extremes in order to advance knowledge. In actual practice, Lamoreaux adds (2015, p. 1252), discussion in both disciplines "tends to push scholars toward the middle of this range." This trend, in part, has been exemplified by the use of citations. Economic historians use more nonintegral citations, as in history, in order to make previous research (rather than authors) prominent, and they also include fewer attributed sources, as in economics, to give more strength to their own claims rather than to those of the cited authors. The idea of a balanced influence from both sides is always present, thus adding to the spatial notion of middle-ground and true hybridization for Economic History.

3.4.3 Science and Technology Studies: The Critical Type

During the 1980s, a different kind of instrumental interdisciplinarity gained priority in science-based areas of economic competition such as computer sciences, biotechnology, manufacturing, and high-technology industries. Weingart (2000, p. 39) labeled these as cases of "strategic" or "opportunistic" interdisciplinarity that serve the needs of the marketplace. Most of these were defined as topical subfields within Science and Technology Studies that met a current market demand (Jasanoff, 2017). They were joined by other examples such as environmental studies, bioethics, science policy, etc. However, these fields, whatever their origins as instrumental or even strategic and opportunistic, seem to have been transformed into sites of critical interdisciplinarity once they were integrated into the realms of Science and Technology Studies.

Science and Technology Studies, as explained by Jasanoff (2013, p. 118), originated under the influence of "multiple, convergent, intellectual and social upheavals" of the later twentieth century. Among those, there was a rise of reflexivity and critical theory as analytical frames and "a postmodern skepticism about power structures and authoritative institutions," which also helps to characterize the field as critical. Within this perspective, the story of Science and Technology Studies can be told as a sequence of struggles: with science and scientists about "its authoritativeness," with established disciplines "about the need for new questions and new methods and discourses with which to address them," and even with its own practitioners about "how far to press the struggle for disciplinary independence" (Jasanoff, 2013, p. 117).

These struggles might help us to understand, in part, the results obtained from the linguistic analysis carried out. As illustrated earlier, the use of integral and nonintegral citations as well as the use of citations to convey attribution or averral in Science and Technology Studies articles resemble their use in the articles from the sciences and technologies, regardless of whether they come from computer engineering or from biomedicine. It seems as if the humanity component, represented by ethics in this case, does not influence the interdiscipline greatly in any of the aspects studied. Thus there is a clear winner of the struggle between ethicists on the one side and scientists and engineers on the other.

According to Mitcham and Nan (2017), ethicists are trying to work with scientists and engineers, and scientists and engineers are experiencing a need to learn from ethicists. Yet – and this might be one explanation for the major influence of the sciences and technologies over the language of the interdiscipline – "the interdisciplinary interaction has remained somewhat externalist, in the sense that Ethics as a discipline has been left largely unaffected by science and technology" (Mitcham and Nan, 2017, p. 253), except when it becomes relevant to scientists, engineers, and the social challenges their work generates. In other words, ethics is considered important only when scientists and engineers need it; it is not considered relevant on its own. Another reason might be that, with respect to science and technology, practitioners are always skeptical that anyone "not trained in a technical field could have legitimate things to say about that field's workings" (Jasanoff, 2017, p. 201). Indeed, many of the earliest practitioners within Science and Technology Studies had postgraduate degrees in science and engineering before entering that field. Thus there is an implicit requirement to be formally qualified in a field in order to speak authoritatively about it (Jasanoff, 2017). Again, the more fine-grained analysis that will be described in Section 4 will help us to visualize the critical dimension of the field better.

To conclude, the analysis carried out in this section has allowed us to compare each interdiscipline with the single-domain fields that interact in each case. Citation density rates were calculated first and two different aspects were studied after that: the visibility (integral vs. nonintegral) and strength (averral vs. attribution) of the external sources. The preliminary conclusions arrived at serve to acknowledge that although citations are similarly frequent or more frequent in interdisciplinary writing when compared with monodisciplinary equivalents, this needs to be further tested on other corpora due to the absence of statistically significant findings for the three cases. A second conclusion is that the values found for the interdisciplines as regards the parameters of visibility and strength always stand in the middle when compared with those of the single-domain fields. Yet this does not mean that the three interdisciplines are similar, since the influence from the various monodisciplines varied considerably in each case, as shown. One possible way to contextualize such differences in this work has been the description of the interdisciplines according to different contrasting typologies introduced by Klein (2017).

4 Interdisciplines Compared: Attribution through Citation in Interdisciplinary Writing

In this section, only the interdisciplinary fields are examined through a more detailed study of citations so as to address the second research question: How does the use of bibliographical citations differ across the three interdisciplines? As this question focuses on the comparison between interdisciplines, no comparison has been made between those and the single-domain disciplines that constitute them. Moreover, and due to the more fine-grained analysis that the selected linguistic aspects demand, some methodological decisions had to be made. More specifically, the scope has been reduced to the analysis of the phenomenon of *attribution through citation* only, which is represented by 1,565 citation tokens in the three interdisciplinary fields. Therefore, none of the cases of *averred citations* in the same fields, which comprise 6,871 citation tokens, were considered here. This reduction in scope was needed because each occurring citation had to be individually analyzed for each of the three dimensions presented and categorized accordingly, a task that would have been difficult to carry out with all occurring citations. At the end of this section, an attempt is also made at contextualizing the findings obtained in the light of different modes of interdisciplinarity (Barry and Born, 2013) that are rooted in epistemological considerations.

Attribution, understood by Murphy (2005, p. 131) as the "transferral of responsibility for what is being said to a third party," always conveys an evaluative process. As pointed out by Hunston (2011, p. 33) "one of the key modifiers of the status of a proposition is its attribution by the writer to another speaker." However, although attribution always modifies status, this might occur in different ways. It can depend on the grammatical structure employed, on the verb used, or on the source type (Hunston, 2011). A variety of grammatical structures have been identified as commonly used in attribution, such as *that*-clauses, structures with *as*, reporting phrases like *according to*, etc. (Hunston, 2011). In addition, the choice of a specific verb affects status, since it "allows the writer either to reclaim that responsibility or to distance him/herself still further" (Hunston, 2011, p. 38). This matter of the responsibility of the other researcher as source (Hunston, 2000) might be also affected depending on text integration (Coffin, 2009) issues; that is, depending on the way in which the attributed proposition is incorporated into the text. Based on these considerations, three aspects will be analyzed in this study of markers of attribution across the three interdisciplines: the types of grammatical structures, the processes of textual integration, and the choices of reporting verbs.

4.1 Grammatical Structures

Hunston (2011, p. 38) proposes a set of grammatical structures typically occurring in cases of attribution, which have been also investigated by Murphy (2005), among others. Most of them have been encountered in the corpus, and they have been initially grouped into three sets: (1) the *that-clause* group; (2) the *as* group; and (3) the *reporting phrases* group.

4.1.1 The That-*Clause Group*

This type of reporting structure, studied in detail by Charles (2006) and Swales (2014), among others, allows for the presence of three main cases: a reporting verb followed by a *that*-clause, as in example (20); a noun followed by a *that*-clause, as in example (21); and an introductory *it* passive structure followed by a *that*-clause, as in example (22):

(20)   Indeed, Walter Scheidel (2012a, p. 11) has argued that "Perhaps the biggest unacknowledged question of Roman economic history is [. . .]." [EH]

(21)   There is also evidence that the serotonergic system is also involved in EFs, in part by influencing the activity of the dopaminergic system (Reuter, Ott, Vaitl, & Henning, 2007). [EN]

(22)   It has been shown repeatedly that by age 3, children begin to learn as well from video presentations as from live presentations in word learning, action imitation, and object search tasks [9,18,20]. [EN]

Another type of passive structure has been found, also acknowledged by Shaw (1992), whose grammatical meaning might implicitly equal a *that*-clause. In these cases, although no *that*-clause explicitly occurs, its implicit meaning does, as in examples (23) and (24):

(23)   Number line estimation performance was found to be associated with arithmetic performance and learning repeatedly [16,5]. [EN]

(24)   Mind wandering has been shown to reduce after mindfulness practice in adults [15]. [EN]

These examples can be rephrased, without their meaning being changed, into sentences like (23a) *It was found that number line estimation performance is associated with [. . .]* or (24a) *It has been shown that mind wandering reduces after mindfulness practice* [. . .]. When this paraphrase is possible, it might be stated that we are in the presence of attribution cases.

4.1.2 The As Group

Two different cases are included here, which are treated together because in both cases *as* is used in combination with a verb. The first case occurs when *as* precedes a finite or nonfinite clause, whether in the active or the passive voice (*as X suggests* or *as suggested by X*), as in examples (25) and (26):

(25)   As Hansson (2007, p. 265) states, "There is a risk that users will feel that they are controlled by this technology, rather than using it themselves to control their surroundings." [STS]

(26)   However, as suggested by Neville Francis and Valerie Ramey (2005), non-technology stocks such as [. . .]. [EH]

A second case occurs when a verb is followed by a noun phrase and a prepositional phrase beginning with *as* (*X describes something as*), as in example (27):

(27)   Similarly, Stovall (2011, p. 110) saw reflexivity as a sort of master virtue that fosters [. . .]. [STS]

4.1.3 The Reporting Phrases Group

These are typical reporting structures like *according to X, for X*, or *in X's words*. The common feature they share is that although it is clear that they are used to attribute somebody else's words or thoughts, no verb is used because the phrases are semantically attributive on their own.

As regards *according to X*, this typical reporting structure has been found throughout the corpus in different cases: as part of an integral citation with a human source, as in example (28); with an abstract-human source, as in example (29); or as part of a nonintegral citation making reference to a nonhuman source, as in example (30).

(28)   According to Harris, "moral paternalism refers to protection of individuals from 'corruption,' moral wickedness, or degradation of a person's character" (1977, 85). [STS]

(29)   According to Estes et al.'s review [14], although formal education appears to discourage thematic thinking this relationship may vary across cultures. [EN]

(30)   According to recent evidence [29], functional features might even be privileged in biological kind classification. [EN]

The expression *for X* is not a very frequent reporting structure in the corpus. When found, it was part of an integral citation (in which the cited author(s) is placed within the grammar of the sentence), as in example (31), or a nonintegral one (in which the cited author(s) is placed within parentheses, square brackets, or superscript numbers) as in example (32):

(31)   For Margulis et al., "chimeras are real. Life is not shy" (2011, 4). [STS]

(32)   For authors in these traditions, human relationality is a precondition for subject-
        ivity, not the other way around (Taylor, 1985; Taylor, 1989; Mackenzie and
        Stoljar, 2000). [STS]

Finally, the expressions *in X's words* or *in the words of X* are not very frequent reporting structures and can be present in two different ways according to the type of possessive construction used: by using a genitive *'s*, as in example (33), or by using the preposition *of*, as in example (34). Typically, these structures are commonly used when a direct quotation is introduced.

(33)   In Clark's words, "did the institutions create the trade in medieval Europe or did
        trade possibilities create their own institutions?"[62] [EH]

(34)   In the words of Temin (2013, p. 236), "The question therefore is not whether
        Malthusian constraints were present, but rather what changes in Roman times led
        to growth within these constraints and how far growth went." [EH]

Although the described three groups count for most of the grammatical structures used for attribution in the corpus, it is important to point out that other cases of attribution, particularly those conveyed by direct quotations, might not always occur as part of the presented types. In other words, if there is a direct quotation, there is always attribution, as pointed out by Thompson (2005, p. 38). Furthermore, direct quotations might be part of *that*-clauses, as in example (20), part of *as*-clauses, as in example (25), or introduced by reporting phrases, as in examples (28), (31), (33), and (34). However, there are still some other cases in which direct quotations do not fit into any of these grammatical resources, which have been included within a fourth group: the *direct quotation* group.

4.1.4 The Direct Quotation Group

Three different variants have been identified within this group from the cases encountered in the corpus. The first variant is typical of cases showing what from a Systemic Functional Linguistics (SFL) perspective might be called projection achieved by means of a "paratactic clause" (Halliday, 1994, pp. 250–72), in which the level of the proposition is "free-standing" (Hunston,

2013, p. 625). Important for the purpose of this section, there is a clear syntactic role for the cited author as a subject, as these examples show:

(35) Gerald Gaus (2005, p. 33) writes: "although we may be able to obtain knowledge of abstract principles of right, particular judgments and specific issues involve conflicting principles, and [thus] it is exceedingly difficult to provide answers to these questions that have any claim to being clear and definitive." [STS]

(36) Thompson (2013, 64) sums this up: "putting these regulations into action, then, is first and foremost about enabling research in an environment of ethical controversy, and not about ethical inquiry." [STS]

(37) Herlihy further generalizes: "the highly skewed distribution of wealth in the fifteenth-century was a comparatively new development, and (...) wealth had been somewhat more evenly distributed across the population in the thirteenth century, before the onslaught of the great epidemics" (Herlihy 1978, p. 139). [EH]

The second variant is illustrated by cases in which, if it were not for the presence of the quotation marks, averral through citation would be the case. In other words, there is not an attributed proposition; rather, the proposition is averred by the current writer. However, attribution exists because there is a direct quotation:

(38) In a very similar vein, Rhodes (2009, 667) proposed an "ethical response to reflexivity that asks questions rather than provides answers; that refuses the hubris of generalizations; that provokes thinking rather than provides answers; that generates possibilities rather than prescriptions; that seeks openness rather than closure." [STS]

(39) She uses the term to describe "a massive demand for but selective access to a form of social welfare based on medical, scientific, and legal criteria that both acknowledge biological injury and compensate for it" (Petryna, 2002, p. 6). [STS]

If a name should be given for those cases, I would suggest the label *quoted averral*. In a sense, cases like this fit into the grey area that Murphy (2005, p. 132) has called "middle ground between averral and attribution." As for the syntactic role of the cited author, it can be explicitly shown to be part of an integral citation, as in example (38), or of a nonintegral one, as in (39).

The case for the third variant is different. I am specifically referring to cases where direct quotations are part of nonintegral citations embedded within the main narrative of the text. The only linguistic resource employed to show attribution is the use of the quotation marks, and the cited author is given no syntactic role at all. I have labelled those cases as *plain direct quotations*.

(40)   However, some parts of northern Europe were slow in doing so. England, in particular, "was unlike many other European countries in having no public precautions against plague at all before 1518" (Slack 1985, p. 201). [EH]

(41)   Domestically, officials saw themselves engaged in an effort to persuade "the masses to internalize appropriate values" (Garon 1997, p. 7). [EH]

It is important to point out that although the three variants have been placed within the same group, because they are all cases in which direct quotations do not fit the main grammatical categories proposed for attribution, they will be not be reported in the same way. On the one hand, the *paratactic* and the *quoted averred* citations will be grouped together under the label *author DQ* (abbreviation for "author's direct quotation") because the cited author performs an explicit syntactic role within the sentence. The *plain direct quotations* (plain DQ), on the other hand, will be reported separately, since no syntactic role at all is given to the cited author.

4.1.5 Presentation of Results

After each of the 1,565 cases of attribution through citations was classified according to the categories proposed above, their distribution across the interdisciplinary sub-corpora was calculated, as shown in Table 4.1 and Figure 4.1.

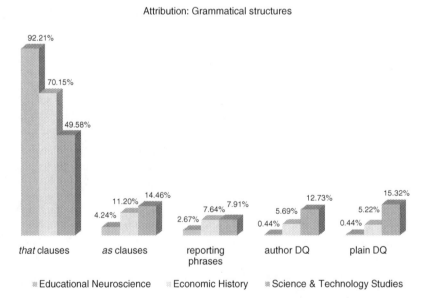

Figure 4.1 Percentage of grammatical structures used for attribution in the three interdisciplines

Table 4.1 Frequency of grammatical structures used for attribution in the three interdisciplines

		That clauses	*As* clauses	Reporting phrases	Author DQ	Plain DQ	Total attributed sources
Educational Neuroscience	tokens	413	19	12	2	2	448
	(%)	92.21%	4.24%	2.67%	0.44%	0.44%	100%
Economic History	tokens	376	60	41	31	28	536
	(%)	70.15%	11.20%	7.64%	5.69%	5.22%	100%
Science and Technology	tokens	288	84	46	74	89	581
Studies	(%)	49.58%	14.46%	7.91%	12.73%	15.32%	100%

Findings show that there is a clear preference for the use of *that*-clauses in the three corpora. This is not surprising, since it has been already acknowledged that this is "the most frequent phraseological pattern used for citations" (Charles, 2006, p. 331). However, differences between the interdisciplines have been found. In Educational Neuroscience, the frequency of *that*-clauses (92.21%) is higher than in Economic History (70.15%) and much higher than in Science and Technology Studies (49.58%). The use of the following structure, phrases with *as*, shows the opposite trend: in Science and Technology Studies, the frequency is higher (14.46%) when compared with Economic History (11.20%) and Educational Neuroscience (4.24%). The difference between both structures and the effects they create on the text have been analyzed in detail by Hunston (2011). The following examples from the corpus will be used to illustrate such differences:

(42)   Santoni de Sio et al. (2014) <u>claim that</u> the possibility of different descriptions of a given activity may be relevant for understanding the impact of performance-enhancing technologies on the nature of care activities. [STS]

(43)   Vallor (2011) <u>describes</u> care activities <u>as</u> a platform for the development of necessary care skills as well as skills for becoming an empathic human being. [STS].

In example (42), the main clause (*Santoni de Sio et al. (2014) claim that*) acts as a modification of the *that*-clause, thus modifying the status of the proposition therein (*the possibility of different descriptions of a given activity ...*). As a result, as Hunston (2011, p. 38) explains, "the writer's own voice is subordinated" to that of Santoni de Sio and his colleagues and might be "overlooked completely." However, when *as*-clauses are used, as in example (43), the writer's voice "as an interpreter" of Vallor's ideas is much stronger (Hunston, 2011, p. 38). Here we go back to the idea that "the writer's voice is stronger where the attribution is not expressed through a *that*-clause" (Hunston, 2011, p. 38). In example (42), the proposition is explicitly attributed to Santoni de Sio and colleagues by means of the *that*-clause, and that is why the cited author's voice is stronger and the writer's voice is more suppressed. In example (43), however, the writer intervenes to interpret and refor-mulate Vallor's ideas, thus suppressing the cited author's voice and making his/her own voice stronger. In other words, "*describing something as ...*" implies a less close paraphrase of the original proposition than "*claims that ...*" does.

Going back to the findings, as Educational Neuroscience writers in the corpus use more *that*-clauses, a tendency might be shown for a subordination of their voices to those of the cited authors in comparison with Economic History writers and even more markedly when compared with Science and Technology Studies writers when attribution is performed. Needless to say, this analysis would be richer if treated in complement with the distinction of different syntactic roles given to the cited authors, whether as syntactic subjects (human or nonhuman) or as part of passive constructions (Thompson and Tribble, 2001), which has not been carried out in this study.

When direct quotations that do not fit any of the grammatical structures are analyzed, whether the cited author is given a syntactic role or not, the opposite trend is observed. These cases are more frequent in Science and Technology Studies (28.05%) in comparison with Economic History (10.91%), and they are even more frequent in comparison with Educational Neuroscience (0.88%). This time, it is not the grammatical status of the proposition that counts but, rather, the "degree of mediation on the part of the writer" (Hunston, 2013, p. 213). It has been previously acknowledged that propositions expressed through direct quotations are the least mediated, thus leading to the representation of the cited author's voice as the most explicit (Flottum et al., 2006). Example (44) is useful to explain this claim:

(44)   Columbus may have discovered a new world in the geographical sense. In reality, Dewey says: "Steam and electricity have done more to alter the conditions under which men associate together than all the agencies which affected human relationships before our time" (Dewey 1954, 323). Dewey argues that these new technologies have contributed more to the establishment of modern democratic forms of government than the political theories of Locke and the utilitarians did. [STS]

The SFL concept of *projection* (Halliday, 1994) is referred to again here to understand these cases. For example, projection can be achieved through the use of paratactic clauses (e.g. *Dewey says: "Steam and electricity . . ."*) or hypotactic clauses (e.g. *Dewey argues that new technologies . . .*). Paratactic constructions, which project "free-standing" propositions, usually introduce direct quotations. In those cases, the mediation of the writer is less than in cases in which *that*-clauses, which project propositions "which are subsidiary to a verbal process," are introduced. Thus there is "progression of mediation on the part of the writer" from the quotation (less mediated) to the reported proposition by means of a *that*-clause (more mediated) (Hunston, 2013, p. 625).

Furthermore, as expressed by Flottum et al. (2006, p. 230), when another author is directly quoted, the writer directly transfers "complete responsibility for the reported sentence," that is, responsibility of content but also of form, as in *Dewey says: "Steam and electricity . . ."* In *Dewey argues that new technologies . . .* the writer also transfers responsibility of content to the author; however, responsibility of form is mediated by the writer. As a result, the degree of explicitness of the cited author's voice is affected. The less mediated an attributed proposition (by using a quotation), the more explicit the author's voice; conversely, the more mediated the attributed proposition (by using a *that*-clause, for example), the less explicit the author's voice.

Looking back at the findings, as Science and Technology Studies writers in the corpus include more direct quotations, we might be able to see a tendency to make the cited author's voices more explicit and their propositions less mediated in comparison with Economic History and in a higher proportion when compared with Educational Neuroscience writers when attribution is performed.

To conclude, it is important to make it clear that the concepts of writer's voice and degree of writer mediation refer to two different phenomena according to the examples analyzed. On the one hand, when introducing a *that*-clause that shows attribution, writers subordinate their voices to those of the external sources; that is, the writers' voices are suppressed. On the other hand, as the projected proposition is not a free-standing one but requires some degree of modification (a reporting verb is needed), such a proposition is more mediated by the writer than one projected by means of a direct quotation. However, a higher degree of mediation on the part of the writer does not mean that his or her voice is less suppressed than that of the cited author or vice versa, since we are referring to two different features.

In the last part of this section, when the preliminary conclusions are presented (Section 4.4), the findings reported here for the types of grammatical structures used will be discussed to enrich the description of the interdisciplines in the light of different modes of interdisciplinarity (Barry and Born, 2013). In Section 4.2, a complete analysis of the textual integration of sources follows, in which all the cases, regardless of the grammatical structure in which they are embedded, are studied according to the way in which they are incorporated into the text.

4.2 Textual Integration of Sources

This dimension of the study of citations has been investigated by several scholars, who have given different names for more or less similar phenomena. Hyland (2000), for example, explored different ways in which source material could be incorporated into the writer's argument and distinguished between *short quotes* (up to six or eight words), *blocks* (extensive use of original wording as indented blocks), *summary* (from a single source), and *generalizations* (where material is ascribed to two or more authors) (Hyland, 2000, p. 26). Before him, Swales (1986, p. 50) used the terms *short* and *extensive* to describe citations that are at a single sentence level or those that encompass more than one sentence, although he did not differentiate between quotations and paraphrases or summaries. Thus a long quotation or a long paraphrase would both be considered *extensive* in Swales's system. More recently, Coffin (2009), based on White (2003), explored the way in which sources are integrated into the text according to different degrees of *textual integration* to find out whether the original utterance is directly quoted or reworded. Coffin (2009) presented three cases: *insertion*, when the writer directly quotes a source;

assimilation, when the writer rewords the referenced proposition by paraphrasing and summarizing; and *insertion + assimilation*, which involves a combination of rewording and direct quotation. The conclusions Coffin (2009) arrives at as regards the rhetorical effects these choices create in the text will be of special interest for the discussion of the findings. The framework adopted for the analysis of the cases, however, is the one introduced by Borg (2000), which has been also applied by Petrić (2012).

Borg (2000, p. 8) proposed a taxonomy of four types of citations: *extended, brief, fragment,* or *paraphrase/summary*. All citations except paraphrase/summary are direct quotations. In other words, if a citation contains quotation marks, it is considered a direct quotation, whether extended, brief, or fragment; if it is not, it is considered a paraphrased/summary citation. It is important to make clear that special attention will be paid to the linguistic mechanisms of direct quotation rather than to the analysis of summary and paraphrasing cases, mainly due to the fact that for the latter to be complete, a detailed study of the different rhetorical functions they perform in the text should be included.

4.2.1 Extended Quotations

An extended quotation is longer than forty words (Borg, 2000) and is typically formatted as a block quotation (Petrić, 2012), as in the following example:

(45)   Finally, even if the IETF were to gain the legitimacy necessary to protect human rights, and decided to enable these through Internet standards and protocols, there is a real risk of (further) Internet fragmentation:

When governments become sufficiently frustrated with the way standards are being designed, or find that the existing standards process no longer serves their national economic or security interests, then we might see a large country like China, or a coalition of countries, decide to abandon the current standards process, effectively cleaving the Internet at the logical layer. (Hill 2013:36) [STS]

4.2.2 Brief Quotations

A brief quotation is a *t*-unit or more, which is shorter than forty words. A *t*-unit is a single independent clause, including all modifying dependent clauses (Crookes, 1990, p. 184). Lee et al. (2018, p. 6) call them "whole clauses." These are some examples:

(46)   The OECD suggested that "an improvement of one-half standard deviation in mathematics and science performance at the individual level implies, by historical experience, an increase in annual growth rates per capita of GDP of 0.87%" ([38], p. 17). [EN]

(47)   The authors conclude: "[...] Media clearly play an important role in the current
        epidemic of childhood and adolescent obesity. The sheer number of advertisements
        that children and adolescents see for junk food and fast food have an effect [...]"
        [9]. [EN]

(48)   According to Humphries (2003, p. 96), "this aspect of the Statute, which distin-
        guished it from continental legislation, perhaps recognized that [...]." [EH]

4.2.3 Fragment Quotations

A fragment is a direct quote that is less than a *t*-unit. In other words, fragments
are short "stretches of textual borrowing" (Petrić, 2012, p. 106) that are "shorter
than a clause such as words and phrases" (Lee et al., 2018, p. 6), as these
examples show:

(49)   The task of principlism is, as Albert Jonsen puts it, to create "the common coin of
        moral discourse" in order, one might add, to help resolve "the cultural tensions"
        created by medical scientific advance (1998, 333). [STS]

(50)   Slave owners, therefore, had "little to gain from improvements in roads," and "no
        particular desire to attract settlers by building schools and villages and factories"
        (Wright 1986, p. 18). [EH]

4.2.4 Paraphrase/Summary Quotations

Borg (2000, p. 8) defines those cases as "another writer's thoughts expressed in
the author's own words, and so needing an overt reference." These citations
always refer to a specific reference, but one that is restated in the writer's own
voice, as explained earlier.

(51)   Further, Rinne, Gregory, Yarmolinskaya, and Hardiman (2011) argue that the arts
        may engage learners in thinking about new information in ways that improve
        retention. [EN]

(52)   As Erik J. Engstrom (2012) has shown, many of these changes affected the
        turnout of voters, and changes in electoral laws explain much of the decline in
        voter turnout in the late nineteenth and early twentieth century. [EH]

4.2.5 Presentation of Results

As before, the 1,565 tokens identified as cases of attribution through citation
have been classified according to the categories presented, and their distribution
across the corpus has been calculated. Findings for every interdisciplinary field
have been summarized in Table 4.2 and Figures 4.2 and 4.3.

Table 4.2 Frequency of textual integration processes in the three interdisciplines

		Summary/ paraphrasing	Fragment DQ	Brief DQ	Extended DQ	Total DQ	Total attributed sources
Educational Neuroscience	tokens	429	7	11	1	19	448
	(%)	95.77%	1.56%	2.45%	0.22%	4.23%	100%
Economic History	tokens	372	93	65	6	164	536
	(%)	69.41%	17.35%	12.12%	1.12%	30.59%	100%
Science and Technology	tokens	242	242	86	11	339	581
Studies	(%)	41.65%	41.65%	14.80%	1.90%	58.35%	100%

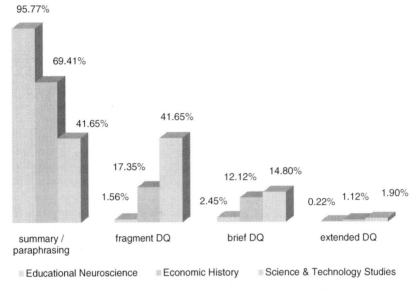

Figure 4.2 Percentage of textual integration processes in the three interdisciplines

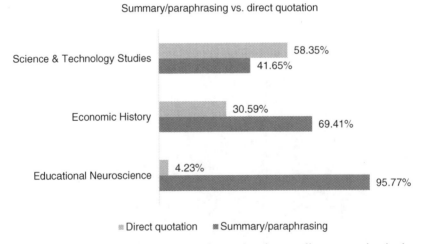

Figure 4.3 Percentage of summary and paraphrasing vs. direct quotation in the three interdisciplines

According to the findings reported, it is clear that there is a preference for integrating sources by means of summary and paraphrasing rather than by direct quotations in Educational Neuroscience (95.77%) when compared with both Economic History (69.41%) and Science and Technology Studies (41.65%). As for the type of direct quotation, both Science and Technology Studies and Economic History writers rely more on *fragment* direct quotations (41.65% and 17.35% respectively), followed by *brief* direct quotations (14.80% and 12.12% respectively) and *extended* direct quotations (1.90% and 1.12% respectively). However, Educational Neuroscience writers prefer *brief* (2.45%) more than *fragment* (1.56%) direct quotations, but the frequencies are very low.

As regards the preferences for summarizing and paraphrasing or direct quoting in different disciplines, previous work has demonstrated that paraphrasing and summarizing is most widely employed in all disciplines. However, in the natural sciences, the frequency of direct quotations is minimal or even nonexistent, while frequencies of up to a third of the total citations have been encountered in the social sciences and the humanities (Dubois, 1988; Pickard, 1995; Hyland, 2000; Thompson, 2005). Thus the most striking finding in the corpus is the fact that the frequency of direct quotations in Science and Technology Studies is higher than the frequency of summary or paraphrasing. In the paragraphs that follow, a more detailed analysis of the mechanisms applied when direct quotations are used will be introduced.

Direct quotation is considered relatively "undemanding" on the part of the writer in comparison to paraphrasing or summarizing, since "it does not require any textual modification of the appropriated material," as pointed out by Petrić (2012, p. 102). However, the level of academic literacy required is greater than commonly thought (Petrić, 2012). Jakobs (2003), as cited by Petrić (2012), makes a distinction between two types of integration processes when incorporating source material into a text: *co-textual* and *contextual*. While *co-textual* integration refers to "the adaptation of text passages to the linguistic co-text," *contextual* integration is concerned with "the adaptation of others' formulations to the present communication context" (Jakobs, 2003, p. 898). Direct quotation requires intervention at these two levels.

At the co-textual or linguistic level, a different vocabulary, syntax, and style are brought into the writer's text. As a result, Petrić (2012) concludes, writers have to carry out different actions in order to successfully incorporate a selected passage into their texts. For example, they need to add transition words, as in examples (53) and (54); omit parts of the quotation to make it fit into their sentences, as in (55); or make different morphological, syntactic, or ortho-graphic changes, as in (56) and (57) (Petrić, 2012).

(53)   While one human genetics researcher writes that "selecting for specific traits" is eugenic, another argues that parents are simply "seeking traits to complement their particular family," or "determin[ing] the number, spacing and quality of their children" (Wertz, Fletcher, and Mulvihill 1991, 1210). [STS]

(54)   Critics have complained, however, that "consigning consideration of legal, ethical and social issues to special agencies" only "compartmentalizes the problems" rather than "encouraging coordinated ethical and scientific inquiry in which each influences the other's development (Cranor 1994, 4). [STS]

(55)   Thus, Rosen (2007, 132) claims that "contemporary biological citizenship, in the advanced-liberal democracies of 'the West' [...], does not take this racialized and nationalized form." [STS]

(56)   More realistically, the news media can be chastised, according to Dorothy Nelkin (1996), for "underplay[ing] the complexity of genetic and environ-mental interactions and ignor[ing] the distance between diagnosis and ther-apy" (p. 30). [STS]

(57)   In her study on German modernization, Mary Nolan (1994) notes that American influences on German entrepreneurship were limited before WWI. But "(w)ith the end of Germany's acute postwar dependency and instability, America came to be seen as an economic model" (p. 38). [EH]

At the contextual level, "quotations may reflect a different purpose and intention, level of writer authority, and context of writing than the sur-rounding text" (Petrić, 2012, p. 103). Thus writers need to frame the quotation in line with their own intentions. For instance, they may add appropriate introductions or comments about the quoted passage or phrase, as in examples (58) and (59), or they may add words to qualify the quotations and signal their stance towards the ideas expressed in the quotation, as in example (60) (Petrić, 2012).

(58)   In a recent article, the bioethicist Hank Greely (2013, 44) asks "have ESCROs been worthwhile?" and his answer is "a strong, definite 'probably.'" [STS]

(59)   The conclusion is that in relations to economics and demography "politics may have played a larger role in determining who might benefit or suffer from

a government's particular vision of the rightful order of things and the 'just price'" (Cohn 2007, pp. 475–76). [EH]

(60)   "It is time to take the 'human' out of human rights." This <u>provocative claim</u> was made by John Harris (2011), a renowned professor of bioethics and director of the Institute for Science, Ethics and Innovation at Manchester University, UK. [STS]

As explained, the adaptation of text passages to the linguistic co-text as well as the adaptation of others' formulations to the specific communication contexts are the two mechanisms underlying the process of direct quotation, especially when brief or fragment quotations are employed. These mechanisms are usually employed by writers in order to signal their stance towards the claims made in the quotations as well as to frame the quotations according to their own intentions. In these cases, a kind of manipulation of the quoted words might be perceived, which specifically serves the writer's purposes.

From a dialogical perspective, as acknowledged by Coffin (2009) based on Martin and White (2005), the choice between summarizing or paraphrasing the cited author's view or quoting him or her directly creates distinct rhetorical effects in the context of academic writing. The rhetorical effect of *assimilation* – that is, when the source material merges into the writer's argument as a summary or paraphrase – is that "the referenced proposition is more likely to be perceived as an established fact, thus creating dialogic contraction," that is, closing down the interchange of alternative views. Quoted wordings, or *insertion*, on the other hand, "make a proposition more open to counter argument by being clearly located as the view of but a single source" (Coffin, 2009, p. 174). The effect produced is that the text becomes more dialogically expansive; that is, more room is left for greater degrees of dialogical exchanges (Coffin, 2009).

As done in Section 3, the findings reported here for the types of textual integration processes involved will be discussed to add to the description of the interdisciplines in the light of different modes of interdisciplinarity (Barry and Born, 2013) when the preliminary conclusions are presented (Section 4.4). In Section 4.3, a detailed analysis follows of the reporting verbs employed to convey attribution through citation in the three cases.

4.3 Reporting Verbs

As already stated, the specific noun or verb chosen in the construction of attribution affects status (Hunston, 2011). Here, only the verbs will be analyzed, based on the abundant previous research carried out on the topic. The use of a reporting verb to introduce the work of other researchers is a significant rhetorical choice. As Charles puts it, this choice is a key feature that enables writers to "position their work in relation to that of other members of the discipline" (Charles, 2006, p. 318). Hunston (1993) points out that the status of the knowledge depends on the kind of verb chosen. The importance of these verbs therefore lies in the fact that they allow the writer to clearly convey the kind of activity reported and to adopt a position towards that information, signaling whether the claims are to be taken as accepted or not (Hyland, 2000). In the following subsections, different available taxonomies will be presented that provide a framework of analysis for the verbs encountered across the corpus.

4.3.1 Classification According to Processes or Activities Involved

Thompson and Ye (1991, pp. 372–3) distinguish three categories of reporting verbs according to the process they perform: *textual* verbs, in which there is an obligatory element of verbal expression (e.g. *state*, *write*); *mental* verbs, which refer to mental processes (e.g. *think*, *believe*); and *research* verbs, which refer to processes that are part of research activity (e.g. *find*, *demonstrate*). Based on those founding categories, Thomas and Hawes (1994, p. 132) present a different classification of the kinds of activities or processes involved. Thus they distinguish between *Discourse Activity* verbs, *Cognition Activity* verbs, and *Real-World or Experimental Activity* verbs. Finally, based on both taxonomies, Hyland (2000, p. 27) developed his own framework and distinguished between three processes: *Research (real-world) Acts*, which might occur in statements of findings or procedures; *Cognition Acts*, which are concerned with mental processes; and *Discourse Acts*, which involve verbal expression.

4.3.2 Classification According to Evaluative Potential

Besides information about the process or activity performed, "writers also exploit the evaluative potential of reporting verbs" (Hyland, 2000, p. 28). Thus writers can vary their commitment to the message by adopting an explicitly personal stance or by attributing a position to the original author. Based on the complex and detailed taxonomy proposed by Thompson and Ye (1991) to count for evaluation in reporting verbs, Hyland (2000, p. 28) presented his own, proposing three ways in which the writer may represent the reported information: as *true* (e.g. *acknowledge, point out, establish*); *false* (e.g. *fail, overlook, exaggerate, ignore*); or *nonfactively*, giving no clear signal. This last option allows the writer to report the source author as *positive* (e.g. *advocate, argue, hold, see*), *neutral* (e.g. *address, cite, comment, look at*), *tentative* (e.g. *allude to, believe, hypothesize, suggest*), or *critical* (e.g. *attack, condemn, object, refute*) (Hyland, 2000).

4.3.3 Classification According to Meaning Groups

Several studies have been carried out adopting the models for analyzing reporting verbs presented in the previous paragraphs. A slightly different approach, however, was adopted by Charles (2006), who analyzed reporting verbs according to *meaning groups* as presented for verb grammar patterns (Francis et al., 1996). For example, she found four main different meaning groups in her data: *argue* verbs, concerned with writing and other forms of communication (e.g. *argue, suggest, assert, point out*); *think* verbs, concerned with processes of thinking, believing, knowing, understanding, hoping, fearing, (e.g. *think, assume, feel*); *show* verbs, concerned with indicating a fact or a situation (e.g. *show, demonstrate, reveal*); and *find* verbs, which are concerned with coming to know or think something (e.g. *find, observe, discover, establish*).

4.3.4 Classification According to Author Roles

Another different approach, although based on the same founding categories, was adopted by Fløttum et al. (2006, p. 215), who posed these questions: "What are the other researchers allowed to do? What roles do the authors assign to the other researchers when relating to them?" In order to address them, they propose four *author roles* according to four different types of reporting verbs. These are: the *writer* role, which is typically manifested by discourse verbs and denotes either processes involving verbal or graphical representation, such as *describe, discuss, illustrate, outline, present, repeat,* and *summarize,* or processes directly related to the text structuring and the guiding of the reader (Dahl, 2004), such as *begin by, focus on, move on, (re)turn to,* and *conclude by*; the *researcher* role, which is typically manifested by research verbs referring to the action or activities directly related to the research process, such as *analyze, assume, consider, choose, compare, explore, find, follow, limit, study, test,* and *use*; the *arguer* role, which is typically manifested by position verbs denoting processes related to position and stance, explicit argumentation concerning approval, promotion, or rejection, such as *argue, claim, dispute, maintain, propose,* and *reject*; and the *evaluator* role, which is typically manifested by evaluation and emotion verbs and verb constructions such as *feel, be content to, be skeptical about, be struck by, find something + evaluative adjective* (Fløttum et al., 2006, p. 216).

4.3.5 Presentation of Results

As regards the cases counted, all verbs occurring in *that*-clauses and in structures with *as*, whether they are part of active or passive constructions, as well as verbs that are part of *paratactic* direct quotations have been analyzed. In other words, the only verbs that have not been counted are those verbs that occur in *quoted averral* cases.

In the first stage, verbs were classified according to the type of activity or process they perform; that is, whether they are *research, mental,* or *discourse* verbs (Thompson and Ye, 1991; Thomas and Hawes, 1994; Hyland, 2000). As no mental verbs occurred among the most frequent ones in any of the three interdisciplines, the distinction was made between discourse and research verbs only. The classification of the verbs according to the type of process or activity they represented did not present major difficulties, since they were all clear examples of typical verbs for each group and most of them appeared as typical examples in the taxonomies provided for Thompson and Ye (1991) and Thomas and Hawes (1994). Only the verbs *reveal, claim,* and *estimate* do not appear as examples in any of those two previous studies. However, Charles (2006, p. 319) classified *claim* and *estimate* within the *argue* group, which she acknowledges "parallels the textual group," and *reveal* as a *show* verb, which, together with the *find* verbs, parallel the research group as described by Thompson and Ye (1991).

A wide variety of reporting verbs are present in the three interdisciplinary corpora. In the case of Educational Neuroscience, thirty-four different verbs (types) were identified, while fifty-six different verbs (types) were found in Economic History. As for Science and Technology Studies, a total of fifty different verbs (types) were encountered. Only verbs occurring ten or more times have been considered for further analysis, since no conclusions could be drawn from those occurring fewer times. The complete list of all the reporting verbs, including those occurring fewer than ten times, can be found in Appendix 2. In each interdisciplinary field, only eight verbs occurred ten or more times; their distribution is reported in Table 4.3 and illustrated in Figures 4.4, 4.5, and 4.6.

Table 4.3 The most frequent reporting verbs in the three interdisciplines

Educational Neuroscience			Economic History			Science and Technology Studies		
verbs	tokens	frequency	verbs	tokens	frequency	verbs	tokens	frequency
show	109	28.54%	argue	72	18.66%	argue	72	25.63%
find	61	15.98%	show	54	13.98%	suggest	33	11.75%
suggest	58	15.18%	suggest	49	12.70%	state	17	6.05%
demonstrate	41	10.73%	note	30	7.77%	point out	16	5.70%
report	23	6.02%	find	29	7.51%	claim	15	5.33%
argue	12	3.14%	conclude	14	3.62%	show	14	4.98%
propose	11	2.88%	point out	12	3.10%	find	13	4.62%
reveal	10	2.61%	estimate	10	2.60%	reveal	11	3.91%
Others	57	14.92%	Others	116	30.06%	Others	90	32.03%
Total	382	100%	Total	386	100%	Total	281	100%

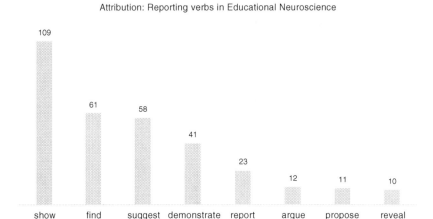

Figure 4.4 The most frequent reporting verbs in Educational Neuroscience

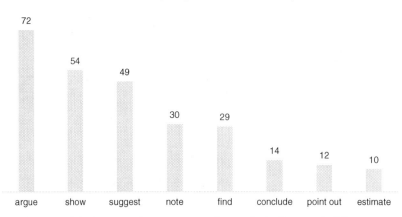

Figure 4.5 The most frequent reporting verbs in Economic History

In Educational Neuroscience, the two most widely used verbs are *show* (28.54%) and *find* (15.98%), which, together with *demonstrate* (10.73%) and *reveal* (2.61%), belong to the research verbs group. A special case is *report* (6.02%), a verb that Thomas and Hawes (1994) have described as a discourse verb. This verb can also be used as a research verb to communicate findings, as acknowledged by Thompson (2001). Indeed, this is the meaning that *report* conveys in all the cases encountered. As a consequence, I have counted it as a research verb. Then, the third most frequently used verb is *suggest* (15.18%),

Attribution: Reporting verbs in Science & Technology Studies

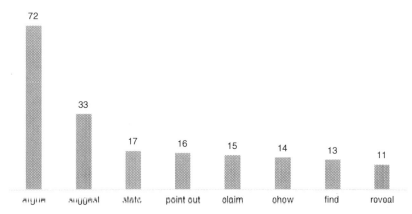

Figure 4.6 The most frequent reporting verbs in Science and Technology Studies

which, together with *argue* (3.14%) and *propose* (2.88%), represent the discourse verbs. If we consider only the most widely used verbs as a new whole, research verbs represent 75.07% of the total while discourse verbs represent the remaining 24.93%.

In Economic History, the verb *argue*, which is a discourse verb, is the most widely used (18.66%). The verbs *suggest* (12.70%), *note* (7.77%), *conclude* (3.62%), *point out* (3.10%), and *estimate* (2.60%) belong to this group. As for research verbs, *show* (13.98%) is the second most widely used verb, and only one more verb with the same meaning, which is *find* (7.51%), belongs to this group. When considering the most widely used verbs as a new whole, discourse verbs represent 69.26% of the total this time, while research verbs account for the remaining 30.74%.

Finally, in Science and Technology Studies, *argue* (25.63%), followed by *suggest* (11.75%), *state* (6.05%), *point out* (5.70%), and *claim* (5.33%), are the five most widely used verbs, all of them discourse verbs. The other three verbs, which are *show* (4.98%), *find* (4.62%), and *reveal* (3.91%), are examples of research verbs. If the most widely used verbs are considered as a new whole, discourse verbs represent 80.10% of them while research verbs represent the remaining 19.90%.

For a clearer understanding of the relationships between the most widely used *research* and *discourse* verbs in the three interdisciplinary fields, these findings have been summarized in Table 4.4 and illustrated in Figure 4.7.

Table 4.4 Most frequent *research* vs. *discourse* verbs in the three interdisciplines

	Educational Neuroscience		Economic History		Science and Technology Studies	
	tokens	frequency	tokens	frequency	tokens	frequency
Research verbs	287	75.07%	118	75.07%	76	19.90%
Discourse verbs	95	24.93%	268	24.93%	305	80.10%
Total verbs	382	100%	386	100%	381	100%

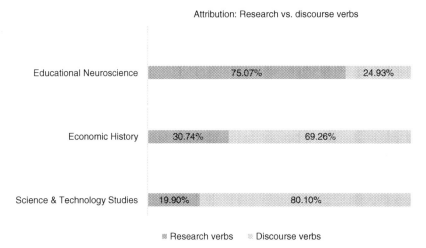

Figure 4.7 Percentage of most frequent *research* vs. *discourse* verbs in the three interdisciplines

It is widely accepted that there is a preference for the natural sciences to use "research type" verbs, while social sciences and humanities largely favor "discourse activity" reporting verbs, as pointed out by Hyland (2000, p. 28). Based on this statement and on the results shown, it can be concluded that researchers in Educational Neuroscience use reporting verbs in similar ways to researchers in the natural sciences. In addition, researchers in Economic History seem to adhere to the norm for the social sciences and the humanities, which is in fact logical due to the nature of both interacting disciplines. Similarly, but in a more marked way, this association with social sciences and humanities is found also for reporting verbs in Science and Technology Studies, where researchers use many more discourse than research verbs.

In a second stage of this analysis, verbs have been studied as regards their evaluative potential. As stated before, reporting verbs can be divided into those that are *factive*, when the writer indicates by such a choice that "she or he believes that the reported proposition is correct," and those which are *nonfactive*, when the writer "makes no such assumption" (Swales, 2014, p. 125). As for the most widely used verbs encountered, all the research verbs are factive: *show*, *find*, *demonstrate*, *reveal*, and *report*. On the other hand, all the discourse verbs are nonfactive except for *point out*, which has been described as factive (Hyland, 2000). According to the results reported in Table 4.3, factive verbs predominate in Educational Neuroscience (63.88%) in comparison with both Economic History (24.59%) and Science and Technology Studies (19.21%), while nonfactive ones predominate in both Science and Technology Studies

(48.76%) and Economic History (45.35%) in comparison with Educational Neuroscience (21.20%).

A final consideration is to be made as regards the kind of *author roles* (Fløttum et al., 2006) these verbs help to perform in each interdiscipline. Because of a higher frequency of research verbs which are also factive (63.88%), it can be argued that cited authors are given the role of *researchers* in Educational Neuroscience. Those researchers report findings and solutions, show results, find facts, and demonstrate effects, as illustrated by the following passages, typically encountered throughout the corpus.

(61)   Previous work by Dweck and colleagues has **demonstrated** that students may hold different core beliefs about the nature of intelligence [6,7]. Research has **shown** that students holding such beliefs [. . .], and research by Aronson et al. [2] **demonstrated** that it is possible to teach incremental theory to college students [. . .] [12]. [EN]

(62)   As Green et al. [18] have **shown**, the rate of temporal discounting is influenced by reward magnitude. [. . .] A recent study by Christakou et al. [5] investigated the neural maturation that accompanies this. They **found** that the previously observed age-related decrease in impulsive choices during adolescence [. . .]. Research by Olson et al. [38] has also **shown** that developing connectivity between networks in the brain [. . .]. They **demonstrated** that discounting behaviour was related to [. . .]. [EN]

As for cited authors in Science and Technology Studies, the high frequency of position verbs like *argue, claim,* or *point out* (36.66%) might help to describe them as performing an *arguer* role, which is typically manifested by the presence of explicit argumentation concerning approval, promotion, or rejection. Some typical intertextual passages like the following, in which the nature of these verbs is reinforced by the whole context (italicized phrases) can serve to illustrate this role:

(63)   The ethics of medical mismanagement has captured the attention of many western scholars. Apart from *critics made earlier* by Diamond and Sigmundson (1997) on the John-Joan case, Lev (2006) also **claims** that the outcome of SAS is highly uncertain as no one can determine nor predict what the child would want in his or her life in the future (Lev 2006). [. . .] In fact, the theory that [. . .], *has remained unclear and unsupported by any studies* (Crouch et al. 2004). There are also claims that despite enhanced surgical techniques, *no decisive evidence has shown this theory to be true* (Creighton and Liao 2004). [. . .] Chase (1999) **argues** that SAS may negatively affect [. . .]. [STS]

Finally, it is not easy to find a role for the cited authors in Economic History. On the one hand, they report findings and show results as researchers do; in fact, *show* (13.98%) is the second most used verb. On the other, and because the verb *argue* (18.66%) is most widely used, they also participate as arguers in discussions about the approval, promotion, or rejection of claims and ideas. However, none of those roles seems to be as marked as the researcher role performed by cited authors in Educational Neuroscience or the arguer role they perform in Science and Technology Studies. In fact, arguments, claims, and findings are moderate, softened perhaps by the high presence of tentative verbs like *suggest* (12.70%). This new blended role can thus be labeled as *arguer/researcher*. Commonly encountered intertextual passages like the following might help to illustrate this role.

(64) [...], previous research **suggests** a downward bias to all of our estimates. Kernell and McDonald (1999) *provide evidence that* Representatives facing competitive elections prior to the establishment of RFD [   ]. This echoes *claims* by Fuller (1964), who **argued** that motivated Representatives [...]. Kernell and McDonald (1999) **point out** that RFD routes eliminated thousands of post office positions. [...] As Erik J. Engstrom (2012) has **shown**, many of these changes affected the turnout of voters, [...]. [EH]

(65) This fits the findings of more detailed studies. Ralf Ritcher and Jochen Streb (2011) quote contemporary sources **reporting** that American machine tools [...]. Ritcher (2011) **concludes** that not only thousands of American machine tools were in use in Germany, but also [...]. In a more recent article, Cristiano Ristuccia and Adam Tooze (2013) analyze [...] and **find** that German additions to the machinery stock [...]. On the basis of *this evidence, they reject the notion* of dichotomous technological paths across the Atlantic, at least in this industry. [EH]

So far, the three interdisciplines under study have been described as regards the ways in which the phenomenon of attribution through citations is inscribed according to three main aspects: the grammatical structures employed, the processes of textual integration applied, and the meanings of the reporting verbs used. It is time now to contextualize the findings obtained in the characterization of each interdisciplinary field according to different modes of interdisciplinarity (Barry and Born, 2013).

4.4 Preliminary Conclusions: Modes of Interdisciplinarity

As stated in the introduction to this work, and based on epistemological concepts, it is possible to identify three modes of interdisciplinarity; that is, three "ideal-typical arrangements of the interrelations between disciplines" (Barry and Born, 2013, p. 34): the *subordination-service* mode, the *integrative-synthesis* mode, and the *agonistic-antagonistic* mode. The claim has been also made that each of the three cases that have been analyzed in this Element might correspond to one of these modes.

4.4.1 Educational Neuroscience: The Subordination-Service Mode

From the articles analyzed in the Educational Neuroscience sub-corpus, it can be suggested that writers in the corpus use *that*-clauses of attribution in a markedly high frequency. In addition, in such articles, the voices of the cited authors are less explicit because of a low frequency of direct quotations, which indicates that the attributed propositions are more mediated by the writer. When incorporating source material into their texts, Educational Neuroscience writers in the corpus seem to have a preference for paraphrasing or summarizing rather than quoting other authors. This type of textual integration has been described by previous researchers (Coffin, 2009; Hu and Wang, 2014; Lee et al., 2018; among several others) as creating a rhetorical effect of dialogical contraction that might tend to close down the possibilities for alternative views. Finally, Educational Neuroscience writers in the corpus use more research than discourse reporting verbs, which are also factive. Because of these verb choices, cited authors adopt the role of researchers. Most of these features have been already acknowledged as typical of the language of the natural sciences. For instance, it has been demonstrated that *that*-clauses are more frequent in the natural sciences than in the social sciences and humanities (Charles, 2006; Hyland, 2000). Educational Neuroscience, however, **is not exactly** a natural science; it is an interdisciplinary construction whose scientific knowledge **comes from** a natural science (neuroscience) but which is also **informed by** a social science (education). Yet the relationship between both disciplines is not one of equality. Rather, it is constructed by subordination and service bonds.

In a *subordination-service* mode of interdisciplinarity, as already explained, one discipline occupies a subordinate or service role in relation to the other discipline. According to this mode, the service discipline is typically conceived as making up for, or filling in for, an absence or lack in the other, which is the master discipline (Barry and Born, 2013). In some cases, the social sciences are understood precisely in such terms. They appear to make it possible for the natural sciences to engage with social factors that had been excluded from analysis or consideration (Marcus, 2002). In Educational Neuroscience, then, education would be the service discipline that makes it possible for neuroscience, which is the master discipline, to engage with social issues. Thus the language adopted is more similar to the language of the natural sciences because this is the master science in the relationship. In other words, it is the one that creates knowledge, although this knowledge is informed by the social science. The kind of knowledge that is produced must be useful for a better understanding of learning from a cognitive or neurobiological perspective. Logically, the processes occurring in our brain and nervous system when learning are described in the same way as other biological processes: informed by previous research that is reported by using language that is typical of those sciences. From a more critical perspective, Penny (2006, n.p.) refers to this kind of interdiscipline as made of "practitioners who are firmly rooted in one discipline" and have "a strong internal sense of its authority," that is, who feel that they hold the "master discourse" through which, as informed by the service discipline, they "exploit or reprocess" its own subject matter. Finally, if neuroscience really wants to contribute to the complex practice of education, a middle road between scientific rigor and a more pragmatic approach must be found (Edelenbosch et al., 2015). As far as attribution is concerned, it is the scientific rigor that has been clearly shown by Educational Neuroscience writers in the studied corpus.

4.4.2 Economic History: The Integrative-Synthesis Mode

According to the findings, Economic History writers in the corpus also use *that*-clauses of attribution most frequently, as shown for all interdisciplines. However, they use more *that*-clauses than Science and Technology Studies writers but fewer than Educational Neuroscience writers. In addition, when incorporating source material into their texts, Economic History writers in the corpus prefer to paraphrase or summarize rather than to quote other authors but in lower degrees when compared with Educational Neuroscience writers. Finally, they use more discourse than research reporting verbs, although the two most widely used verbs are from each group. Because of these verb choices, cited authors adopt a blended role between researchers and arguers, as they combine reports of findings with the approval, promotion, or rejection of claims and ideas. In general terms, most of these features have been acknowledged as characterizing the language of the soft sciences (as referred to by Hyland, 2000), which include both social sciences and humanities. This is, in fact, logical, since Economic History is an interdisciplinary formation made up of knowledge constructions that come from both types of disciplines.

According to the findings reported, every time a linguistic aspect of attribution was analyzed – that is, grammatical structures, textual integration, and reporting verbs – Economic History figures stood in the middle between those of Educational Neuroscience and Science and Technology Studies. This might be taken as evidence that the way in which the disciplines involved in Economic History interact is different from both Educational Neuroscience and Science and Technology Studies. Indeed, no master or service discipline has been encountered, nor a purely critical-reflective one either. What has been described, instead, is a hybrid or "interstitial cross-discipline" (Klein, 2017, p. 27) that springs from an *integrative-synthesis* mode. According to this mode, interdisciplinary work is defined as "integrating and negotiating knowledge and modes of thinking from two or more disciplines" (Barry and Born, 2013, p. 24). Such work, then, aims at advancing understanding; that is, explaining phenomena, finding solutions, or raising new questions in ways that would have not been possible through single-disciplinary means (Boix Mansilla and Gardner, 2003).

This interdisciplinary integration not only occurs between economics and history but also across other interdisciplinary connections that are synthesized in the new hybrid discipline. This is so because disciplines are not monads (Osborne, 2013). Indeed, there is always a certain degree of transparency or porosity. The social sciences, Osborne (2013, p. 134) suggests, "are especially porous in their aptitude for certain kinds of mobility across, and cross-fertilization with, other areas of inquiry." In the case of Economic History, for example, mathematics, statistics, or computer studies are disciplines that cross boundaries across the social sciences to inform computer-based models and methods of statistical projection that economic historians use in their studies. This last fact might serve to help us understand why Economic History writers in the corpus make their cited authors *argue* and *suggest* but also *show* and *find*.

4.4.3 Science and Technology Studies: The Agonistic-Antagonistic Mode

The findings reported suggest that Science and Technology Studies writers in the corpus use *that*-clauses of attribution most frequently, as writers in all interdisciplines do, but they also make use of other resources, like quoting averred statements or introducing plain quotations in their arguments. Thus the cited authors' voices are more explicit and the attributed propositions are less mediated by the writer. As they use more direct quotation than summary or paraphrasing, a rhetorical effect of dialogical expansion (Martin and White, 2005) is created, thus leading to more spaces for dialogic exchange. Finally, writers use more discourse than research verbs and a high proportion of position verbs and, because of these choices, cited authors adopt the role of arguers. Most of these features have been acknowledged as typical of the discourse of the soft sciences (Hyland, 2000), which includes both social sciences and humanities. Science and Technology Studies, however, relies on the humanities only to exercise its **critical reflection** upon the power of science and technology on the society. Such subject matter, however, originates in the hard sciences (Hyland, 2000), represented here by the natural sciences and the technologies.

As stated before, Jasanoff (2013) acknowledges the existence of an *agonistic-antagonistic* relationship between Science and Technology Studies and existing or prior forms of disciplinary knowledge and practice. According to this mode, interdisciplinarity arises from the dialogue around, criticism of, or opposition to the limits of established disciplines, as already stated (Barry and Born, 2013). For Penny (2006), when a new discipline comes in as an outsider to another discipline with a different set of values, the fundamental assumptions by which that discipline is structured are revealed. This kind of interdisciplinarity, Penny (2006, n.p.) concludes, can be fruitful in "enabling a context for the mutual critique of the fundamental assumptions of the different disciplines." That is why Science and Technology Studies research opens up science, technology, and society to "critical assessment and interrogation" (Felt et al., 2017, p. 1).

In order to critically reflect upon the relationships between science, technology, and society, Science and Technology Studies writers need to make use of a language that allows them to criticize, evaluate, question, or negotiate with different views, positions, and claims. When attributing other sources, writers in the corpus seem to use a language which is similar to the language of soft disciplines in general. However, some hints that denote a more critical orientation have been observed. For example, Science and Technology Studies writers in the corpus use more direct quotations than paraphrasing, which is even unusual for social sciences and humanities. Moreover, they do it by quoting fragments most of the time, for which different processes of textual and contextual adaptations are needed. This kind of manipulation of the quoted words helps them to signal their personal stance towards the claims made in the quotations according to their own purposes. At the same time, by making extensive use of direct quotations, writers bring external voices explicitly into their own arguments, which opens up more spaces for dialogue and negotiation, which is typical of the nature of this interdiscipline. This effect is strengthened by giving those cited authors a positional role of arguers. In sum, when Science and Technology Studies writers in the corpus attribute other sources, they do it by using linguistic resources that continuously enhance critical reflection.

To conclude, from the analysis of the articles that make up the present corpus it can be argued that the language of attribution used by Science and Technology Studies writers shares similarities with the language of the soft disciplines but with some glimpses of a more critical touch. As for the language used to convey attribution by Economic History writers, it can be depicted as typical of the more moderate soft disciplines with some glimpses of scientific rigor. This scientific rigor, which is characteristic of the hard disciplines, is most strongly present in the language of attribution used by Educational Neuroscience writers.

The analysis carried out in this section has allowed the comparison of the three interdisciplinary fields in the light of three linguistic aspects within the phenomenon of attribution through citation: the types of grammatical structures, the processes of textual integration, and the choices of reporting verbs. The findings obtained from the study of these aspects have suggested that disciplinary knowledge forms interact in different ways in each interdiscipline. In other words, the interrelations between disciplines is different for each case. One possible way to contextualize such differences in this work has been the description of each interdiscipline according to the different modes of interdisciplinarity introduced by Barry and Born (2013).

5 Conclusions: Interdisciplinary Complexity, Pluralism, and Ambiguity

The research in this Element is based on the premise that disciplinary differences can be reflected by linguistic differences and, by the same token, linguistic differences can signify disciplinary differences. The main aim has been to describe linguistic differences across interdisciplinary fields; this is challenging, since from the outset, fixed theoretical preconceptions needed to be overcome in order to understand a different way of conceptualizing academic knowledge. From the simple definition of what a discipline is to the complex interweaving of academic cultures, epistemic natures, and disciplinary subject matter, everything must be scrutinized under a different lens. What is needed when language is the focus is a magnifying glass: interdisciplinary footprints are spread all around.

As already acknowledged, the three interdisciplinary fields studied were chosen *a priori* precisely because they were different from an epistemological point of view: they could be described as representing different types and modes of interdisciplinarity. These types and modes are useful to describe the ways in which interdisciplinary research and practices are carried out, but they do not describe the role language plays in them. They are rooted in epistemic notions, not in linguistic ones. Thus it was necessary to look for linguistic evidence of these interdisciplinary practices in the texts themselves. It was found that, indeed, the interdisciplinary fields are also different from a linguistic point of view, as might be inferred from the summarized conclusions as follows.

In this exploratory, corpus-based case study, three different interdisciplinary fields have been compared in the light of the study of bibliographical citations.

These features have also been analyzed in the interdisciplines in comparison with the single-domain disciplines involved in each case. The results lead to three main conclusions. First, that bibliographical citations are likely to be similarly frequent or more frequent in interdisciplinary writing when compared with monodisciplinary writing. However, and due to the absence of statistically significant findings for all the cases, this hypothesis needs to be further tested on other and larger corpora. If supported, this finding suggests that, when writing for interdisciplinary audiences, writers not only make use of a broader range of previous literature but also of a more extensive one. The second conclusion is that values found for the linguistic features analyzed in the interdisciplines stand in the middle when compared with the single-domain fields. However, this does not mean that we are in the presence of identical interdisciplines, since the influence from one or the other single-domain fields varies considerably in each case. The third conclusion is that the kind of relationship between the single-domain disciplines is different in each interdisciplinary field.

In Educational Neuroscience articles, the study of the visibility of the projecting sources and the strength given to external voices helps to suggest that a gap between education and neuroscience exists, despite the efforts of both educators and neuroscientists to build the bridge, although a somewhat closer resemblance between education and Educational Neuroscience articles can be observed. When citations that convey attribution are analyzed in all their aspects, a different relationship is perceived. It seems to be quite clear, according to the findings, that Educational Neuroscience articles in the corpus follow the conventions of the natural sciences. Rooted in the hierarchical division of labor of the disciplines, a subordination-service relationship arises, which shows the power of practitioners who are firmly rooted in one discipline, which is neuroscience in this case, over practitioners who interact from a subordinated discipline, represented by education in this case.

In Science and Technology Studies articles, the study of the visibility of the projecting sources and the strength given to external sources serves to indicate that they strongly resemble articles from the sciences and technologies, whether they come from computer engineering or biomedicine. The influence of ethics, a critical discipline by nature, is not reflected as much. It seems as if the instrumental origins of the field still exert a greater influence over its critical endeavour. The criticality of the interdiscipline does become apparent, however, when the cases of attribution through citation are explored. Results here suggest that Science and Technology Studies writers in the corpus not only make use of the conventions of the social sciences and humanities but also adopt unusual linguistic features that strengthen the critical orientation of their discourse, which in turn characterizes an agonistic-antagonistic mode of interdisciplinarity. This means an interdiscipline that is based on the dialogue with criticism of or opposition to the limits of established disciplines, all aspects which are only made visible under the lens of ethics.

Finally, when Economic History articles were explored, results from the study of the visibility of the projecting sources show that Economic History articles resemble history more than economics ones. However, as regards the emphasis given to external sources, they show a greater resemblance to economics articles. In other words, the influence of both monodisciplines is balanced in the articles from the corpus, adding to the description of Economic History as a hybrid, interstitial cross-discipline. A similar effect is created when citations that convey attribution are analyzed: common linguistic features of both economics and history are encountered together with the spatial notion of middle ground, typical of an integrative-synthesis mode. What is more, the values observed for Economic History are always midway between the other two interdisciplines. It might be concluded that we are in the presence of a default kind of interdisciplinarity here, one in which the principles of integration and merging of features are truly achieved.

These preliminary conclusions only constitute starting points to open up a debate about which linguistic resources are more prone to show disciplinary differences when the object of study is interdisciplinary writing. Bibliographical citations constitute only one aspect of the multiple ones that could be explored, and, because of that, the findings obtained cannot represent the whole of what is going on in interdisciplinary texts, nor can they be taken as parameters for generalization, since, as already explained, this is an exploratory case study. What is true, however, is that they are common linguistic resources that are used in different ways, and they might serve to provide linguistic evidence to describe the interaction between disciplines in the matrix of inter-disciplinary fields. Viewed in this way, the study of citations constitutes one path to look for interdisciplinary footprints in texts. If in future research other interdisciplinary fields are studied, the extent to which research on bibliograph-ical citations might stand as a proxy for interdisciplinary writing could be evaluated. Finally, a reflection on interdisciplinarity and its core epistemic values is needed in order to understand this research contribution as a whole. These values are the complexity of interdisciplinary knowledge, the appreci-ation of pluralism, and the tolerance of ambiguity.

Knowledge today is depicted as a network with multiple connections. It is best described as a complex "dynamic system" rather than as a "linear structure." Isolated modes of work are replaced by "affiliations, coalitions, and alliances," and older values of "control, mastery, and expertise" are reformulated as "dia-logue, interaction, and negotiation" (Klein, 2004, p. 3). Complexity, thus, is at the basis of interdisciplinarity and offers a more adequate way of approaching knowledge in the twenty-first century, when the world is also an interconnected dynamic mass (Welch, 2011). An interdisciplinary approach treats reality the way it is, with its inherent complexity, rather than taking things apart and separating them. And that is why, according to Welch (2014, n.p.), "disciplinary silos are cracking," or perhaps they are becoming more semipermeable.

As interdisciplinarity embraces complexity, it is also naturally pluralistic. Pluralism is inherent to the idea of interdisciplinarity (Welch, 2011). Epistemological pluralism, as already defined, can be understood as "the holistic amalgamation of insights from diverse perspectives" (Welch, 2011, p. 23). This means that in interdisciplinary research, knowledge is approached "as the tangled web it is," and we understand that truth comes from participating in this web rather than "anchoring it to some static, absolutist framework" (Welch, 2011, p. 23). Epistemological pluralism, as a result, also embraces ambiguity (Newell, 2007; Wolfe and Haynes, 2003). Interdisciplinary practitioners are fundamentally tolerant of ambiguity (Bromme, 2000; Hursh et al., 1983). What is more, they seek out ambiguity while trying to develop interdisciplinary integration (Welch, 2011).

Welch (2014) explains that dealing with this plurality of ideas and the ambiguity this produces requires a disruption of the comfort zone. That means more flexibility and adaptability, which gives a "chameleon aspect" to the concept of interdisciplinarity and a sense of "epistemological vertigo and unsettlement" to its practitioners (Welch, 2014, n.p.). He adds that this aversion to unpredictability has a long history, since our entire philosophical tradition is based upon trying to get rid of uncertainty. In interdisciplinary research, as multiple perspectives need to be dealt with, unsettlement is inevitable. There are different ways of looking at reality, different belief systems, different ideologies, etc., which inevitably clash (Welch, 2014).

The way in which this linguistic research has been carried out, as well as the preliminary findings obtained, add to this sense of ambiguity and unsettlement that is proper to interdisciplinary thinking. When interdisciplinary articles were compared with monodisciplinary ones, the influences exerted by the single-domain fields were studied from the **outside** of the interdisciplinary matrix, since findings from one side were compared with those from the other side in relation to the interdiscipline. This approach was also complemented by a more fine-grained analysis of the single-domain disciplines and their relationships **within** each interdiscipline as part of a single matrix. The results obtained from each approach, however, were different, as already explained. For instance, it turned out that Educational Neuroscience articles resemble education texts more when interdisciplinary and monodisciplinary articles were compared, but they show more similarities with the natural sciences in general when only attribution was studied. Also, Science and Technology Studies articles are more similar to biomedicine and computer engineering texts as regards visibility and strength of sources, but they resemble articles from the humanities more when attribution was explored. For Economic History, more uniformity was observed in both analyses, and a balanced influence from economics and history was encountered. This ambiguity in the reporting of the findings might be seen as a signal that the inherent pluralism of interdisciplinarity and its consequent ambiguity can be also reflected by linguistic aspects.

As for the sense of unsettlement that interdisciplinary practitioners experience, a similar feeling is perceived from the perspective of the corpus linguist. After decades of relying on authoritative previous literature on cross-disciplinary analysis of language features, finding a way to explore interdisciplinary knowledge is not an easy task. Here, the disruption of the comfort zone for the researcher is multiple. First, a different theoretical framework needs to be developed – one that departs from the distinction of disciplinary differences rooted in fixed taxonomies that has been so widely applied for linguistic analysis. Second, different methodological decisions need to be taken. Although still relying on a comparative approach, what to compare and how to compare it deserve special attention. Furthermore, the ambiguity that might result from such comparisons adds to that sense of unsettlement and uncertainty.

To conclude, if corpus-based studies on interdisciplinary discourse are to offer a fresh perspective on the research agenda, the epistemological vertigo that is typical of interdisciplinarity needs to be grasped from a linguistics point of view too. Getting our comfort zones disrupted, adhering to pluralism and flexibility, and accepting the ambiguity these changes convey are the only ways to linguistically navigate interdisciplinary complexity.

Let us give it a chance.

Appendix 1

These are the research articles referred to in this Element:

Set 1

Educational Neuroscience Articles

Dommett, E., Devonshire, I., Sewter, E., and Greenfield, S. (2013). The impact of participation in a neuroscience course on motivational measures and academic performance. *Trends in Neuroscience and Education*, 2, 122–38.

Ferrara, K., Hirsh-Pasek, K., Newcombe, N., Michnick Golinkoff, R., and Shallcross Lam, W. (2011). Block talk: spatial language during block play. *Mind, Brain, & Education*, 5(3), 143–51.

Hardiman, M., Rinne, L. and Yarmolinskaya, J. (2014). The effects of arts integration on long-term retention of academic content. *Mind, Brain, & Education*, 8(3), 144–8.

James, K. and Engelhardt, L. (2012). The effects of handwriting experience on functional brain development in pre-literate children. *Trends in Neuroscience and Education*, 1, 32–42.

Kolinsky, R., Monteiro-Plantin, R., Mengarda, E., Grimm-Cabral, L., Scliar-Cabral, L., and Morais, J. (2014). How formal education and literacy impact on the content and structure of semantic categories. *Trends in Neuroscience and Education*, 3, 106–21.

Kubesch, S., Walk, L., Spitzer, M., Kammer, T., Lainburg, A., Heim, R., and Hille, K. (2009). A 30-minute physical education program improves students' executive attention. *Mind, Brain, & Education*, 3(4), 235–42.

Lee, N., Krabbendam, L., Dekker, S., Boschloo, A., de Groot, H., and Jolles, J. (2012). Academic motivation mediates the influence of temporal discounting on academic achievement during adolescence. *Trends in Neuroscience and Education*, 1, 43–8.

Link, T., Moeller, K., Huber, S., Fischer, U., and Nuerk, H. (2013). Walk the number line: an embodied training of numerical concepts. *Trends in Neuroscience and Education*, 2, 74–84.

Moriguchi, Y. and Hiraki, K. (2014). Neural basis of learning from television in young children. *Trends in Neuroscience and Education*, 3, 122–7.

Sanger, K. and Dorjee, D. (2016). Mindfulness training with adolescents enhances metacognition and the inhibition of irrelevant stimuli: evidence from event-related brain potentials. *Trends in Neuroscience and Education*, 5, 1–11.

Spitzer, U. and Hollmann, W. (2013). Experimental observations of the effects of physical exercise on attention, academic and prosocial performance in school settings. *Trends in Neuroscience and Education*, 2, 1–6.

Education

Maine, F. and Hofmann, R. (2016). Talking for meaning: the dialogic engagement of teachers and children in a small group reading context. *International Journal of Educational Research*, 75, 45–56.

Uitto, M., Kaunisto, S., Kelchtermans, G., and Estola, E. (2016). Peer group as a meeting place: reconstructions of teachers' self-understanding and the presence of vulnerability. *International Journal of Educational Research*, 75, 7–16.

Neuroscience

Lu, Y., Zhong, F., Wang, X., Li, Z., Zhu, Z., King, X., Zhao, J., and Wu, Q. (2015). Mechanism of motilin-mediated inhibition on voltage-dependent potassium currents in hippocampal neurons. *Neuroscience*, 284, 374–80.

Pisu, M., Garau, A., Boero, G., Biggio, F., Pibiri, B., Rore, R., Locci, V., Paci, E., Porsu, P., and Serra, M. (2016). Sex differences in the outcome of juvenile social isolation on HPA axis function in rats. *Neuroscience*, 320, 172–82.

Set 2
Economic History Articles

Alfani, G., Murphy, T., and Hilt, E. (2017). Plague and lethal epidemics in the pre-industrial world: economic history, historical analysis, and the "new history of capitalism". *Journal of Economic History*, 17(2), 1–26.

Aston, J. and Di Martino, P. (2017). Risk, success, and failure: female entrepreneurship in late Victorian and Edwardian England. *Economic History Review*, 70(3), 837–58.

Drixler, F. (2016). Hidden in plain sight: stillbirths and infanticides in Imperial Japan. *Journal of Economic History*, 76(3), 651–96.

Harper, K. (2016). People, plagues, and prices in the Roman world: the evidence from Egypt. *Journal of Economic History*, 76(3), 803–39.

Hilt, E. (2017). Economic history, historical analysis, and the "new history of capitalism". *Journal of Economic History*, 77(02), 1–26.

Kallioinen, M. (2017). Inter-communal institutions in medieval trade. *Economic History Review*, 70(4), 1131–52.

Perlman, E. and Sprick Schuster, S. (2016). Delivering the vote: the political effect of free mail delivery in early twentieth century America. *Journal of Economic History*, 76(3), 769–802.

Salisbury, L. (2017). Women's income and marriage markets in the United States: evidence from the Civil War pension. *Journal of Economic History*, 77(1), 1–38.

Timmer, M., Veenstra, J., and Woltjer, P. (2016). The Yankees of Europe? A new view on technology and productivity in German manufacturing in the early twentieth century. *Journal of Economic History*, 76(3), 874–908.

Watanabe, S. (2016). Technology shocks and the Great Depression. *Journal of Economic History*, 76(3), 909–33.

Zeev, N., Mokyr, J., and Van der Beek, K. (2017). Flexible supply of apprenticeship in the British Industrial Revolution. *Journal of Economic History*, 77(1), 208–50.

History

Piller, E. (2016). German child distress, US humanitarian aid and revisionist politics, 1918–24. *Journal of Contemporary History*, 51(3), 453–86.

Scott, C. (2017). Renewing the "special relationship" and rethinking the return of cultural property: The Netherlands and Indonesia, 1949–79. *Journal of Contemporary History*, 52(3), 646–68.

Thomas, M. (2017). Political violence in the republican zone of Spain during the Spanish Civil War: evolving historiographical perspectives. *Journal of Contemporary History*, 52(1), 140–47.

Set 3

Science and Technology Studies Articles

Borensein, J. and Arkin, R. (2016). Robotic nudges: the ethics of engineering a more socially just human being. *Science & Engineering Ethics*, 22, 31–46.

Cath C, and Floridi L. (2017). The design of the Internet's architecture by the Internet Engineering Task Force (IETF) and human rights. *Science & Engineering Ethics*, 23(2), 449–68.

Gogoll, J. and Müller, J. (2017). Autonomous cars: in favor of a mandatory ethics setting. *Science & Engineering Ethics*, 23, 681–700.

Heinemann, T. and Lemke, T. (2014). Biological citizenship reconsidered: the use of DNA analysis by immigration authorities in Germany. *Science, Technology, & Human Values*, 39(4), 488–510.

Hinterberger, A. (2020). Regulating estrangement: human animal chimeras in postgenomic biology. *Science, Technology, & Human Values*, 45(6), 1065–1086. First Published December 26, 2016.

Keulartz, J., Schermer, M., Korthals, M., and Swierstra, T. (2004). Ethics in technological culture: a programmatic proposal for a pragmatist approach. *Science, Technology, & Human Values*, 29(1), 3–29.

Prainsack, B. (2018). The "we" in the "me": solidarity and health care in the era of personalized medicine. *Science, Technology, & Human Values*, 43(1), 21–44.

Rabino, I. (2003). Genetic testing and its implications: human genetics researchers grapple with ethical issues. *Science, Technology, & Human Values*, 28(3), 365–402.

Salim, M. and Noor, S. (2015). Islamic bioethical deliberation on the issue of newborns with disorders of sex development. *Science & Engineering Ethics*, 21, 429–40.

Salter, B. and Salter, C. (2007). Bioethics and the global moral economy: the cultural politics of human embryonic stem cell science. *Science, Technology, & Human Values*, 32(5), 554–81.

Santoni de Sio, F. and van Wynsberghe, A. (2016). When should we use care robots? The nature-of-activities approach. *Science & Engineering Ethics*, 22, 1745–60.

Steen, M. (2015). Upon opening the black box and finding it full: exploring the ethics in design practices. *Science, Technology, & Human Values*, 40(3), 389–420.

Vaisman, N. (2018). The human, human rights, and DNA identity tests. *Science, Technology, & Human Values*, 43(1), 3–20.

Zhu, Q. and Jesiek, B. (2017). A pragmatic approach to ethical decision-making in engineering practice: characteristics, evaluation criteria, and implications for instruction and assessment. *Science & Engineering Ethics*, 23, 663–79.

Biomedicine

Lim, C. and Suzuki, K. (2016). Systemic inflammation mediates the effects of endotoxemia in the mechanisms of heat stroke. *Biology and Medicine*, 9(1), 1–3.

Sukrama D., Wihandani D., and Manuaba, A. (2016). Topical binahong (*Anredera cordifolia*) leaf extract increases interleukin-6 and VEGF during burn wound healing in Wistar rats infected with Pseudomonas aeruginosa. *Biology & Medicine*, 9(1), 1–6.

Computer Engineering

Bhat, A. (2017). Scope of deep learning in medical image analysis: a survey. *International Journal of Advanced Research in Computer Engineering & Technology (IJARCET)*, 6(8), 1218–23.

Appendix 2

This is the list of all occurring reporting verbs in the interdisciplinary sub-corpus.

Educational Neuroscience			Economic History			Science and Technology Studies		
verbs	tokens	frequency	verbs	tokens	frequency	verbs	tokens	frequency
show	109	28.53%	argue	72	18.65%	argue	72	25.62%
find	61	15.97%	show	54	13.99%	suggest	33	11.74%
suggest	58	15.18%	suggest	49	12.69%	state	17	6.05%
demonstrate	41	10.73%	note	30	7.77%	point out	16	5.69%
report	23	6.02%	find	29	7.51%	claim	15	5.34%
argue	12	3.14%	conclude	14	3.63%	show	14	4.98%
propose	11	2.88%	point out	12	3.11%	find	13	4.63%
reveal	10	2.62%	estimate	10	2.59%	reveal	11	3.91%
observe	8	2.09%	indicate	8	2.07%	observe	8	2.85%
state	6	1.57%	claim	8	2.07%	indicate	7	2.49%
point out	5	1.31%	state	7	1.81%	write	6	2.14%
conclude	4	1.05%	report	7	1.81%	propose	5	1.78%
claim	3	0.79%	demonstrate	7	1.81%	explain	5	1.78%
establish	3	0.79%	emphasize	6	1.55%	remark	4	1.42%
assert	3	0.79%	believe	5	1.30%	put	4	1.42%
confirm	2	0.52%	stress	5	1.30%	stress	3	1.07%

Word	Count	%
assume	2	0.52%
consider	2	0.52%
maintain	2	0.52%
highlight	2	0.52%
think	2	0.52%
explain	2	0.52%
prove	2	0.52%
note	1	0.26%
comment	1	0.26%
accept	1	0.26%
postulate	1	0.26%
posit	1	0.26%
mention	1	0.26%
express	1	0.26%
discover	1	0.26%
emphasize	1	0.26%

Word	Count	%
observe	5	1.30%
assume	3	0.78%
put	3	0.78%
acknowledge	3	0.78%
reveal	3	0.78%
write	3	0.78%
predict	2	0.52%
propose	2	0.52%
posit	2	0.52%
discuss	2	0.52%
know	2	0.52%
contend	2	0.52%
mention	2	0.52%
confirm	2	0.52%
hypothesize	2	0.52%
calculate	2	0.52%

Word	Count	%
believe	3	1.07%
assume	3	1.07%
report	3	1.07%
emphasize	2	0.71%
mention	2	0.71%
contend	2	0.71%
detail	2	0.71%
describe	2	0.71%
conclude	2	0.71%
acknowledge	2	0.71%
opine	2	0.71%
recommend	2	0.71%
comment	1	0.36%
notice	1	0.36%
see	1	0.36%
discuss	1	0.36%

(cont.)

Educational Neuroscience			Economic History			Science and Technology Studies		
verbs	tokens	frequency	verbs	tokens	frequency	verbs	tokens	frequency
			remember	1	0.26%	advise	1	0.36%
			insist	1	0.26%	illustrate	1	0.36%
			recognize	1	0.26%	lay out	1	0.36%
			hint	1	0.26%	like	1	0.36%
			underline	1	0.26%	insist	1	0.36%
			admit	1	0.26%	coin	1	0.36%
			add	1	0.26%	maintain	1	0.36%
			hold	1	0.26%	complain	1	0.36%
			warn	1	0.26%	express	1	0.36%
			express	1	0.26%	demonstrate	1	0.36%
			maintain	1	0.26%	hypothesize	1	0.36%
			complain	1	0.26%	know	1	0.36%
			depose	1	0.26%	note	1	0.36%
			allege	1	0.26%	say	1	0.36%

feel	1	0.26%
inform	1	0.26%
outline	1	0.26%
specify	1	0.26%
say	1	0.26%
consider	1	0.26%
remark	1	0.26%
think	1	0.26%
agree	1	0.26%
Total	386	100.00%

reflect	1	0.36%
surmise	1	0.36%
admit	1	0.36%
Total	281	100.00%

Total	382	100.00%

References

Afifi, T. (2017). Interdisciplinary journals. In M. Allen, ed., *The SAGE Encyclopedia of Communication Research Methods*. Thousand Oaks: Sage, pp. 758–61.

Ansari, D. and Coch, D. (2006). Bridges over troubled waters: education and cognitive neuroscience. *Trends in Cognitive Sciences*, 10(4), 146–51.

Anthony, L. (2017). AntFileConverter (Version 1.2.1) [Computer Software]. Tokyo: Waseda University. Available from www.laurenceanthony.net /software.

Anthony, L. (2018). AntConc (Version 3.5.7) [Computer Software]. Tokyo: Waseda University. Available from www.laurenceanthony.net/software.

Atkinson, D. (2004). Contrasting rhetorics/contrasting cultures: why contrastive rhetoric needs a better conceptualization of culture. *Journal of English for Academic Purposes*, 3, 277–89.

Baker, D., Salina, D., and Eslinger, P. (2012). An envisioned bridge: schooling as a neurocognitive developmental institution. *Developmental Cognitive Neuroscience*, 2(1), 6–17.

Barry, A. and Born, G. (2013). *Interdisciplinarity: Reconfigurations of the Social and Natural Sciences*. London: Routledge.

Beauchamp, C. and Beauchamp, M. (2013). Boundary as bridge: an analysis of the educational neuroscience literature from a boundary perspective. *Educational Psychology Review*, 25(1), 47–67.

Becher, T. (1981). Towards a definition of disciplinary cultures. *Studies in Higher Education*, 6(2), 109–22.

Becher, T. (1987). Disciplinary discourse. *Studies in Higher APPENDIXcation*, 12, 261–74.

Becher, T. and Trowler, P. (2001). *Academic Tribes and Territories*, 2nd ed. Buckingham: Society for Research into Higher Education and Open University Press.

Berkenkotter, C. and Huckin, T. (1995). *Genre Knowledge in Disciplinary Communication: Cognition/Culture/Power*. Hillsdale: Erlbaum.

Biber, D. (1990). Methodological issues regarding corpus-based analyses of linguistic variation. *Literary and Linguistic Computing*, 5(4), 257–69.

Biber, D. (1993). Representativeness in corpus design. *Literary and Linguistic Computing*, 8(4), 243–57.

Biber, D. (1995). *Dimensions of Register Variation: A Cross-Linguistic Comparison*. Cambridge: Cambridge University Press.

Biber, D., Conrad, S., and Reppen, R. (1998). *Corpus Linguistics: Investigating Language Structure and Use*. Cambridge: Cambridge University Press.

Biber, D., Conrad, S., Reppen, R., Byrd, P., and Helt, M. (2002). Speaking and writing in the university: a multidimensional comparison. *TESOL Quarterly*, 36(1), 9–48.

Biglan, A. (1973). The characteristics of subject matter in different academic areas. *Journal of Applied Psychology*, 57(3), 195–203.

Bloch, J. (2010). A concordance-based study of the use of reporting verbs as rhetorical devices in academic papers. *Journal of Writing Research*, 2, 219–44.

Boix Mansilla, V. and Gardner, H. (2003). Assessing interdisciplinary work at the frontier: an empirical exploration of symptoms of quality. Paris: CNRS and Institute Nicod. Retrieved from www.interdisciplines.org.

Bondi, M. (2015). Probably most important of all: importance markers in academic and popular history articles. In N. Groom, M. Charles, and S. John, eds., *Corpora, Grammar and Discourse: In Honour of Susan Hunston*. Amsterdam: John Benjamins, pp. 161–82.

Borg, E. (2000). Citation practices in academic writing. In P. Thompson, ed., *Patterns and Perspectives: Insights into EAP Writing Practices*. Reading: University of Reading, pp. 27–45.

Bowers, J. (2016). Psychology, not educational neuroscience, is the way forward for improving educational outcomes for all children: reply to Gabrieli (2016) and Howard-Jones et al. (2016). *Psychological Review*, 123(5), 628–35.

Brezina, V. (2018). *Statistics in Corpus Linguistics: A Practical Guide*. Cambridge: Cambridge University Press.

Bromme, R. (2000). Beyond one's own perspective: the psychology of cognitive interdisciplinarity. In P. Weingart and N. Stehr, eds., *Practising Interdisciplinarity*. Toronto: University of Toronto Press, pp. 115–33.

Bruer, J. (1997). Education and the brain: a bridge too far. *Educational Researcher*, 26(8), 4–6.

Bruer, J. (2017). Points of view: on the implications of neuroscience research for science teaching and learning: are there any? *Life Sciences Education*, 5, 104–10.

Bruun, H., Hukkinen, J., Huutoniemi, K., and Klein, J. (2005). *Promoting Interdisciplinary Research: The Case of the Academy of Finland*. Helsinki: Academy of Finland.

Campbell, S. (2011). Educational neuroscience: motivations, methodology, and implications. *Educational Philosophy and Theory. Special Issue: Educational Neuroscience*, 43(1), 7–16.

Canagarajah, S. (2002). *A Geopolitics of Academic Writing*. Pittsburgh: University of Pittsburgh Press.

Carew, T. and Magsamen, S. (2010). Neuroscience and education: an ideal partnership for producing evidence-based solutions to guide 21st century learning. *Neuron*, 67(5), 685–8.

Carter, R. (2004). *Language and Creativity: The Art of Common Talk*. London: Routledge.

Centre for Corpus Research (2017). *Preparing to write for an interdisciplinary audience*. University of Birmingham: Elsevier Publishing Campus.

Charles, M. (2003). "This mystery . . .": a corpus-based study of the use of nouns to construct stance in theses from two contrasting disciplines. *Journal of English for Academic Purposes*, 2(4), 313–26.

Charles, M. (2006). Phraseological patterns in reporting clauses used in citation: a corpus-based study of theses in two disciplines. *English for Specific Purposes*, 25, 310–31.

Charles, M. and Pecorari, D. (2016). *Introducing English for Academic Purposes*. London: Routledge.

Choi, S. and Richards, K. (2017). *Interdisciplinary Discourse: Communicating across Disciplines*. London: Palgrave.

Coffin, C. (2009). Incorporating and evaluating voices in a film studies thesis. *Writing & Pedagogy*, 1, 163–93.

Crookes, G. (1990). The utterance and other basic units for discourse analysis. *Applied Linguistics*, 11(1), 183–99.

Cuthbert, A. (2015). Neuroscience and education: an incompatible relationship. *Sociology Compass*, 9(1), 49–61.

Dahl, T. (2004). Textual metadiscourse in research articles: a marker of national culture or of academic discipline? *Journal of Pragmatics*, 36(10), 1807–25.

Dubois, B. (1988). Citation in biomedical journal articles. *English for Specific Purposes*, 7, 181–93.

Dudley-Evans, T. (1986). Genre analysis: an investigation of the introduction and discussion sections of MSc dissertations. In M. Coulthard, ed., *Talking about Text*. Birmingham: University of Birmingham, English Language Research, pp. 128–45.

Duff, P. (2018). Case study research in applied linguistics. In L. Litosseliti, ed., *Research Methods in Linguistics*, 2nd ed. London: Bloomsbury, pp. 305–30.

Edelenbosch, R., Kupper, F., Krabbendam, L., and Broerse, J. (2015). Brain-based learning and educational neuroscience: boundary work. *Mind, Brain, and Education*, 9(1), 40–49.

Feak, C. and Swales, J. (2009). *Telling a Research Story: Writing a Literature Review*. Ann Arbor: Michigan University Press.

Felt, U., Rayvon, C., and Miller, L. (2017). *The Handbook of Science and Technology Studies*. Cambridge, MA: MIT.

Fischer, K., Goswami, U., and Geake, J. (2010). The future of educational neuroscience. *Mind, Brain, & Education*, 4(2), 68–80.

Fløttum, K., Dahl, T., and Kinn, T. (2006). *Academic Voices: Across Languages and Disciplines*. Amsterdam: John Benjamins.

Flowerdew, L. (2004). The argument for using English specialized corpora to understand academic and professional settings. In U. Connor and T. Upton, eds., *Discourse in the Professions: Perspectives from Corpus Linguistics*. Amsterdam: John Benjamins, pp. 11–13.

Francis, G., Hunston, S., and Manning, E. (1996). *Collins COBUILD Grammar Patterns 1: Verbs*. London: HarperCollins.

Frickel, S. (2004). Building an interdiscipline: collective action framing and the rise of genetic toxicology. *Social Problems*, 51(2), 269–87.

Frodeman, R., Klein, J., and Pacheco, R. (2017). *The Oxford Handbook of Interdisciplinarity*, 2nd ed. New York: Oxford University Press.

Fuchsman, K. (2012). Interdisciplines and interdisciplinarity: political psychology and psychohistory compared. *Issues in Integrative Studies*, 30, 128–54.

Gabrieli, J. (2016). The promise of educational neuroscience: comment on Bowers (2016). *Psychological Review*, 123, 613–19.

Gardner, P. (1995). The relationship between technology and science: some historical and philosophical reflections. *International Journal of Technology and Design Education*, 5(1), 1–33.

Graff, H. (2015a). Undisciplining knowledge: interview with Harvey Graff. Retrieved from www.insidehighered.com/news/2015/09/10/author-discusses-new-book-interdisciplinarity.

Graff, H. (2015b). *Undisciplining Knowledge: Interdisciplinarity in the Twentieth Century*. Baltimore: Johns Hopkins University Press.

Groom, N. (2000). Attribution and averral revisited: three perspectives on manifest intertextuality in academic writing. In P. Thompson, ed., *Patterns and Perspectives: Insights for EAP Writing Practice*. Reading: CALS, University of Reading, pp. 15–26.

Groom, N. (2005). Patterns and meaning across genres and disciplines: an exploratory study. *Journal of English for Academic Purposes*, 4(3), 257–77.

Halliday, M. (1994). *An Introduction to Functional Grammar*, 2nd ed. London: Arnold.

Halliday, M. and Martin, J. (1993). *Writing Science: Literacy and Discursive Power*. Pittsburgh: University of Pittsburgh Press.

Halliday, M. and Matthiessen C. (2004). *An Introduction to Functional Grammar*. London: Edward Arnold.

Harwood, N. (2005). "Nowhere has anyone attempted . . . In this article I aim to do just that": a corpus-based study of self-promotional I and we in academic writing across four disciplines. *Journal of Pragmatics*, 37, 1207–31.

Harwood, N. (2009). An interview-based study of the functions of citations in academic writing across two disciplines. *Journal of Pragmatics*, 41, 497–518.

Harwood, N. and Petrić, B. (2012). Performance in the citing behaviour of two student writers. *Written Communication*, 29, 55–103.

Harwood, N. and Petrić, B. (2013). Task requirements, task representation, and self-reported citation functions: an exploratory study of a successful L2 student's writing. *Journal of English for Academic Purposes*, 12, 104–24.

Hood, S. (2011). Writing discipline: comparing inscriptions of knowledge and knowers in academic writing. In F. Christie and K. Maton, eds., *Disciplinarity: Functional Linguistic and Sociological Perspectives*. London: Continuum, pp. 106–28.

Hopkins, A. and Dudley-Evans, T. (1988). A genre-based investigation of the discussion sections in articles and dissertations. *English for Specific Purposes*, 7, 113–21.

Hu, G., and Wang, G. (2014). Disciplinary and ethnolinguistic influences on citation in research articles. *Journal of English for Academic Purposes*, 14, 14–28.

Hunston, S. (1993). Professional conflict: disagreement in academic discourse. In M. Baker, G. Francis, and E. Tognini-Bognelli, eds., *Text and Technology: In Honour of John Sinclair*. Amsterdam: John Benjamins, pp. 115–34.

Hunston, S. (1994). Evaluation and organization in a sample of written academic discourse. In M. Coulthard, ed., *Advances in Written Text Analysis*. London: Routledge, pp. 191–218.

Hunston, S. (2000). Evaluation and the planes of discourse: status and value in persuasive texts. In S. Hunston and G. Thompson, eds., *Evaluation in Text: Authorial Stance and the Construction of Discourse*. Oxford: Oxford University Press, pp. 176–207.

Hunston, S. (2002). *Corpora in Applied Linguistics*. Cambridge: Cambridge University Press.

Hunston, S. (2004). "It has rightly been pointed out . . .": attributions, consensus and conflict in academic English. In M. Bondi, L. Gavioli, and M. Silver, eds., *Academic Discourse: Genre and Small Corpora*. Rome: Officina Edizioni, pp. 15–33.

Hunston, S. (2011). *Corpus Approaches to Evaluation: Phraseology and Evaluative Language*. London: Routledge.

Hunston, S. (2013). Systemic functional linguistics, corpus linguistics, and the ideology of science. *Text & Talk*, 33(4–5), 617–40.

Hursh, B., Haas, P., and Moore, M. (1983). An interdisciplinary model to implement general education. *Journal of Higher Education*, *54*(1), 42–49.

Hyland, K. (1999). Academic attribution: citation and the construction of disciplinary knowledge. *Applied Linguistics*, 20, 341–67.

Hyland, K. (2000). *Disciplinary Discourses: Social Interactions in Academic Writing*. London: Longman.

Hyland, K. (2012). *Disciplinary Identities: Individuality and Community in Academic Writing*. Cambridge: Cambridge University Press.

Hyland, K. (2015). Corpora and written academic English. In D. Biber and R. Reppen, eds., *The Cambridge Handbook of English Corpus Linguistics*. Cambridge: Cambridge University Press, pp. 292–308.

Hyland, K. and Bondi, M. (2006). *Academic Discourse across Disciplines*. Bern: Peter Lang.

Jakobs, E. (2003). Reproductive writing: writing from sources. *Journal of Pragmatics*, 35(893), 906.

Jasanoff, S. (2013). Fields and fallows: a political history of STS. In A. Barry and G. Born, eds., *Interdisciplinarity: Reconfigurations of the Social and Natural Sciences*. London: Routledge, pp. 99–118.

Jasanoff, S. (2017). A field of its own: the emergence of Science and Technology Studies. In R. Frodeman, J. Klein, and R. Pacheco, eds., *The Oxford Handbook of Interdisciplinarity*, 2nd ed. Oxford: Oxford University Press, pp. 191–205.

Kagan, J. (2009). *The Three Cultures: Natural Sciences, Social Sciences and the Humanities in the 21st Century*. New York: Cambridge University Press.

Klein, J. (1996). *Crossing Boundaries: Knowledge, Disciplinarities, and Interdisciplinarities*. Charlottesville: University Press of Virginia.

Klein, J. (2004). Interdisciplinarity and complexity: an evolving relationship. *E: CO*, 6(1), 2–10.

Klein, J. (2005). *Humanities, Culture, and Interdisciplinarity: The Changing American Academy*. Albany: State University of New York Press.

Klein, J. (2010). *Creating Interdisciplinary Campus Cultures: A Model for Strength and Sustainability*. San Francisco: Jossey-Bass.

Klein, J. (2017). A taxonomy of interdisciplinarity. In R. Frodeman, J. Klein, and R. Pacheco, eds., *The Oxford Handbook of Interdisciplinarity*, 2nd ed. Oxford: Oxford University Press, pp. 15–30.

Koester, A. (2010). Building small specialized corpora. In A. O'Keeffe and M. McCarthy, eds., *The Routledge Handbook of Corpus Linguistics*. London: Routledge, pp. 66–79.

Lamoreaux, N. (2015). The future of Economic History must be interdisciplinary. *Journal of Economic History*, 75, 1151–7.

Lee, D. (2010). What corpora are available? In A. O'Keeffe and M. McCarthy, eds., *The Routledge Handbook of Corpus Linguistics*. London: Routledge, pp. 107–21.

Lee, J., Hitchcock, C., and Casal, J. (2018). Citation practices of L2 university students in first-year writing: form, function, and stance. *Journal of English for Academic Purposes*, 33, 1–11.

Manathunga C. and Brew, A. (2012). Beyond tribes and territories: new metaphors for new times. In P. Trowler, M. Sanders, and V. Bamber, eds., *Tribes and Territories in the 21st Century: Rethinking the Significance of Disciplines in Higher Education*. London: Routledge, pp. 44–56.

Marcus, G. (2002). Intimate strangers: the dynamics of (non) relationship between the natural and human sciences in the contemporary US university. *Anthropological Quarterly*, 75(3), 519–26.

Martin, J. (2011). Bridging troubled waters: interdisciplinarity and what makes it stick. In F. Christie and K. Maton, eds., *Disciplinarity: Functional Linguistic and Sociological Perspectives*. London: Continuum, pp. 35–61.

Martin, J. and White, P. (2005). *The Language of Evaluation: Appraisal in English*. New York: Palgrave Macmillan.

McEnery, T., Xiao, R., and Tono, Y. (2006). *Corpus Based Language Studies: An Advanced Resource Book*. London: Routledge.

Merriam, S. (2009). *Qualitative Research: A Guide to Design and Implementation*. San Francisco: John Wiley.

Mitcham, C. and Nan, W. (2017). Interdisciplinarity in ethics. In R. Frodeman, J. Klein, and R. Pacheco, eds., *The Oxford Handbook of Interdisciplinarity*, 2nd ed. New York: Oxford University Press, pp. 241–54.

Moon, R. (1998). *Fixed Expressions and Idioms in English: A Corpus-Based Approach*. Oxford: Clarendon.

Murakami, A., Thompson, P., Hunston, S., and Vajn, D. (2017). "What is this corpus about?" Using topic modelling to explore a specialised corpus. *Corpora*, 12(2), 243–77.

Murphy, A. (2005). Markers of attribution in English and Italian opinion articles: a comparative corpus-based study. *ICAME Journal*, 29, 131–50.

Myers, G. (1990). *Writing Biology: Texts in the Social Construction of Scientific Knowledge*. Madison: University of Wisconsin Press.

Newell, W. (2007). Decision-making in interdisciplinary studies. In G. Morçöl, ed., *Handbook of Decision Making*. Boca Raton: CRC/Taylor & Francis, pp. 245–64.

Oakey, D., Mathias, P., and Thompson, T. (2011). Improving inter-professional communication in health and social care: levels and types of cooperation, corpus linguistics and professional practice. Paper presented at the First Interdisciplinary Conference on Applied Linguistics and Professional Practice. University of Cardiff, Wales, June 23, 2011.

O'Keeffe, A. (2006). *Investigating Media Discourse*. London: Routledge.

O'Keeffe, A., McCarthy, M., and Carter, R. (2007). *From Corpus to Classroom: Language Use and Language Teaching*. Cambridge: Cambridge University Press.

Osborne, T. (2013). Inter that discipline! In A. Barry and G. Born, eds., *Interdisciplinarity: Reconfigurations of the Social and Natural Sciences*. London: Routledge, pp. 82–98.

Patton, K. and Campbell, S. (2011). Introduction: educational neuroscience. *Educational Philosophy and Theory*, 43(1), 1–6.

Peacock, M. (2014). Modals in the construction of research articles: a cross-disciplinary perspective. *Ibérica*, 27, 143–64.

Penny, S. (2006). Interview with Simon Penny. University of California, Irvine.

Petrić, B. (2012). Legitimate textual borrowing: direct quotation in L2 student writing. *Journal of Second Language Writing*, 21, 102–17.

Petts, J., Owens, S., and Bulkeley, H. (2008). Crossing boundaries: interdisciplinarity in the context of urban environments. *Geoforum*, 39, 593–601.

Pickard, V. (1995). Citing previous writers: what can we say instead of "say"? *Hong Kong Papers in Linguistics and Language Teaching*, 18, 89–102.

Pickering, S. and Howard-Jones, P. (2007). Educators' views on the role of neuroscience in education: findings from a study of UK and international perspectives. *Mind, Brain, & Education*, 1(3), 109–13.

Rayson, P. (2017). Log-likelihood and effect size calculator. Retrieved May 18, 2020 from http://ucrel.lancs.ac.uk/llwizard.html.

Repko, A. and Szostak, R. (2017). *Interdisciplinary Research: Process and Theory*, 3rd ed. Los Angeles: SAGE.

Repko, A., Szostak, R., and Buchberger, M. (2017). *Introduction to Interdisciplinary Studies*, 2nd ed. Thousand Oaks: SAGE.

Ritter, H. and Horn, T. (1986). Interdisciplinary history: a historiographical review. *The History Teacher*, 19(3), 427–48.

Schwartz, D., Blair, K., and Tsang, J. (2012). How to build educational neuroscience: two approaches with concrete instances. *British Journal of Educational Psychology Monograph Series II*, 8, 9–27.

Shanahan, M. (2015). Discipline identity in economic history: reflecting on an interdisciplinary community. *Arts & Humanities in Higher Education*, 14(2), 181–93.

Shaw, P. (1992). Reasons for the correlation of voice, tense, and sentence function in reporting verbs. *Applied Linguistics*, 13(3), 302–19.

Sigman, M., Peña, M., Goldin, A., and Ribeiro, S. (2014). Neuroscience and education: prime time to build the bridge. *Nature Neuroscience*, 17(4), 497–502.

Silver, M. (2003). The stance of stance: a critical look at ways stance is expressed and modeled in academic discourse. *Journal of English for Academic Purposes*, 2(4), 359–74.

Sinclair, J. (1988). Mirror for a text. *Journal of English and Foreign Languages*, 1, 15–44.

Stake, R. (1995). *The Art of Case Study Research*. Thousand Oaks: SAGE.

Stubbs, M. (2001). Texts, corpora, and problems of interpretation: a response to Widdowson. *Applied Linguistics*, 22(2), 149–72.

Swales, J. (1986). Citation analysis and discourse analysis. *Applied Linguistics*, 7, 39–56.

Swales, J. (1990). *Genre Analysis: English in Academic and Research Settings*. Cambridge: Cambridge University Press.

Swales, J. (2004). *Research Genres: Exploration and Applications*. Cambridge: Cambridge University Press.

Swales, J. (2014). Variation in citational practice in a corpus of student biology papers: from parenthetical plonking to intertextual storytelling. *Written Communication*, 31, 118–41.

Tadros, A. (1993). The pragmatics of text averral and attribution in academic texts. In M. Hoey, ed., *Data, Description, Discourse*. London: Harper Collins, pp. 98–114.

Teich, E. and Holtz, M. (2009). Scientific registers in contact: an exploration of the lexicogrammatical properties of interdisciplinary discourses. *International Journal of Corpus Linguistics*, 14 (4), 524–48.

Thomas, S. and Hawes, T. (1994). Reporting verbs in medical journal articles. *English for Specific Purposes*, 13(2), 129–48.

Thompson, G. and Ye, P. (1991). Evaluation in the reporting verbs used in academic papers. *Applied Linguistics*, 12(4), 365–82.

Thompson, P. (2001). A pedagogically-motivated corpus-based examination of PhD theses: macrostructure, citation practices and uses of modal verbs. Unpublished PhD thesis, University of Reading.

Thompson, P. (2005). Aspects of identification and position in intertextual references in PhD theses. In E. Tognini-Bonelli and G. Del Lungo

Camiciotti, eds., *Strategies in Academic Discourse*. Amsterdam: John Benjamins, pp. 31–50.

Thompson, P. (2012). Achieving a voice of authority in PhD theses. In K. Hyland and C. Sancho-Guinda, eds., *Stance and Voice in Academic Writing*. Basingstoke: Palgrave MacMillan, pp. 119–33.

Thompson, P. (2015). Writing for an interdisciplinary audience: corpus perspectives [Powerpoint slides]. Talk given at the Federal University of Santa Catarina, Florianopolis, Brazil, April 15, 2016.

Thompson, P. and Hunston, S. (2020). *Interdisciplinary Research Discourse: Corpus Investigations into Environment Journals*. London: Routledge.

Thompson, P. and Tribble, C. (2001). Looking at citations: using corpora in English for academic purposes. *Language Learning & Technology*, 5, 91–105.

Thompson, P., Hunston, S., Murakami, A., and Vajn, D. (2017). Multidimensional analysis, text constellations, and interdisciplinary discourse. *International Journal of Corpus Linguistics*, 22(2), 153–86.

Tognini-Bonelli, E. (2001). *Corpus Linguistics at Work*. Amsterdam: John Benjamins.

Trowler, P. (2012). Disciplines and interdisciplinarity: conceptual groundwork. In P. Trowler, M. Sanders, and V. Bamber, eds., *Tribes and Territories in the 21st Century: Rethinking the Significance of Disciplines in Higher Education*. London: Routledge, pp. 5–29.

Trowler, P. (2013). Depicting and researching disciplines: strong and moderate essentialist approaches. *Studies in Higher Education*, 39(10), 1720–31.

Trowler, P., Saunders, M., and Bamber, R. (2012). *Tribes and Territories in the 21st Century: Rethinking the Significance of Disciplines in Higher Education*. London: Routledge.

Weingart, P. (2000). Interdisciplinarity: the paradoxical discourse. In P. Weingart and N. Stehr, eds., *Practising Interdisciplinarity*. Toronto: University of Toronto Press, pp. 25–41.

Weingart, P. and Stehr, N. (2000). *Practising Interdisciplinarity*. Toronto: University of Toronto Press.

Welch, J. (2011). The emergence of interdisciplinarity from epistemological thought. *Issues in Integrative Studies*, 29, 1–39.

Welch, J. (2014). Mary Jo Ragan Lecture on Interdisciplinary Studies 2014. University of Science and Arts of Oklahoma. Retrieved from www.youtube.com/watch?v=S8egjjkiHss.

White, P. (2003). Beyond modality and hedging: a dialogic view of the language of intersubjective stance. *Text, Special Edition on Appraisal*, 23(3), 259–84.

Willis, J. (2008). Building a bridge from neuroscience to the classroom. *Phi Delta Kappan*, 89(6), 424–7.

Wolfe, C. and Haynes, C. (2003). Interdisciplinary writing assessment profiles. *Issues in Integrative Studies*, 21, 126–69.

Cambridge Elements ☰

Corpus Linguistics

Susan Hunston
University of Birmingham

Professor of English Language at the University of Birmingham, UK. She has been involved in Corpus Linguistics for many years and has written extensively on corpora, discourse, and the lexis-grammar interface. She is probably best known as the author of *Corpora in Applied Linguistics* (2002, Cambridge University Press). Susan is currently coeditor, with Carol Chapelle, of the Cambridge Applied Linguistics series.

Advisory Board

Professor Paul Baker, *Lancaster University*
Professor Jesse Egbert, *Northern Arizona University*
Professor Gaetanelle Gilquin, *Université Catholique de Louvain*

About the Series

Corpus Linguistics has grown to become part of the mainstream of Linguistics and Applied Linguistics, as well as being used as an adjunct to other forms of discourse analysis in a variety of fields. It continues to become increasingly complex, both in terms of the methods it uses and in relation to the theoretical concepts it engages with. The Cambridge Elements in Corpus Linguistics series has been designed to meet the needs of both students and researchers who need to keep up with this changing field. The series includes introductions to the main topic areas by experts in the field as well as accounts of the latest ideas and developments by leading researchers.

Cambridge Elements$^{\equiv}$

Corpus Linguistics

Elements in the Series

Multimodal News Analysis across Cultures
Helen Caple, Changpeng Huan and Monika Bednarek

Doing Linguistics with a Corpus: Methodological Considerations for the Everyday User
Jesse Egbert, Tove Larsson and Douglas Biber

Citations in Interdisciplinary Research Articles
Natalia Muguiro

A full series listing is available at: www.cambridge.org/corpuslinguistics